LIVE INTUITIVELY:
JOURNAL THE WISDOM OF YOUR SOUL

Empowering Your Intuitive Voice !

Love, Candess

Raves about *Live Intuitively: Journal the Wisdom of your Soul*

It's a good thing that our intuition, meaning, and purpose awaken from a great and persistent desire to deepen; deepening into our innate intuition that is our birthright and soul gift through Candess M. Campbell's process using Soul Stems to activate our intuition! I'm pragmatic so using a practical, simple process that works is paramount. You can use your inner intuition to heal and align with the outcome you desire in life. You will be surprised by what rushes out of your fingertips to nurture, heal, and guide you to your North Star. Soul Stems are an effective process to activate intuition and open up to joy!

~ **Carol Hilgers**
Founder | *www.tranquille.net*

I have not read a book so activating and soul stirring as "Live Intuitively," since Natalie Goldberg's "Writing Down the Bones." This book is for everyone, and it will re-vitalize and invigorate even the most seasoned of writers. Fun, challenging and ridiculously "cut to the chase" practical. I know this will be a classic and standard tool for understanding the deepest parts of yourSelf.

~ **Cheyenne Mendel**, Acupuncturist, Bazi Practitioner
https://cheyennemendel.wordpress.com
Crestone, Colorado

Live Intuitively: Journal the Wisdom of Your Soul *by Candess Campbell, PhD is one of the most empowering and insightful books I have come across. It takes you on a journey into the depths of your own process and invites you to dance with your intuitive self and uncover the wisdom within. This book has rekindled my love for writing from my heart! I look forward to sharing this book and process with my clients.*

~ **Katie Cavanaugh**
Speaker, Mentor, Coach for Intrepid Women in Business
http://katiecavanaugh.com

Candess Campbell has written a book that anyone can use to develop their intuition and their health. So often our early childhood programming has sublimated our intuition, and with it our health. Live Intuitively suggests "soul stems" for us to use to journal. Observations on the chakras, and their impact on your physical, chemical and emotional health can be added to your soul stem to create a personalized tool. Her journaling process will take you back through layers of consciousness to get in touch with your original mind, your intuition.

Live Intuitively is a guide book. It is clear and simple. Best of all, once you reach your destination with a soul stem, there is another stem waiting for you. The book could last a lifetime, because our journey back to our intuitive self always lasts a lifetime. Recommended for seekers everywhere.

~ **Patrick Dougherty**,
Holistic Chiropractor 2110 N. Washington Street, Suite One
Spokane WA 99205
www.spokane-chiropractic.com

Live Intuitively:
Journal the Wisdom
of your Soul

CANDESS M. CAMPBELL, PHD

Dedication

To all who bare their souls in their
sacred journals so they can activate their wisdom
and make empowered choices in order to Live Intuitively.

FOREWORD

THERE IS OFTEN one sentence in a book that grabs me and becomes the anchor for the balance of what I recall from it. In reading *Live Intuitively: Journal the Wisdom of Your Soul*, this happened very early in the book, as Dr. Campbell noted, "For years I have been tailoring Soul stems for clients to heal the issues they present, and to assist them to stand firmly and unquestionably on their path to success."

Although the author takes a deep and broad path to bring readers to this reality, she stays firmly infused with that passion in her delivery. Drawing on the power and empowerment of journaling activities, the best-selling author brings her own 40 years experience to assist the reader to "do the work" and find the benefits of experiencing intuitive soul connections and healing.

Add creative meditation, a study of the chakras, a process that allows flexibility, and Soul Stems—or writing prompts—the reward is a book that takes each reader on a directed and very personalized journey of intimate discovery and healing.

Our lives have myriad levels we must explore, and many of them have to be brought to a point of congruence before we can master life's challenges and embrace our intuition in order to then master our quest for being all we have the potential to become... Live Intuitively is an undergirding that develops that congruency.

Work and career, creativity, spirituality, play, health, safety, relationships, and money; self-love, trust, communication, forgiveness, ethics and courage... Dr. Campbell leaves no stone unturned as she leads readers through a time-tested process.

A gifted teacher, Candess Campbell, steps up to shape spiritual growth in a practical and straightforward style. Her work empowers readers to trust their intuition to overcome life's challenges. Her gift and promise to you is a simple, yet poignant book about healing and transforming lives as you learn to cultivate a deep relationship with your intuition and release fear, doubt and resistance in a quest to live fully in the NOW.

What I personally hope for readers is that they find, as has Dr. Campbell, their journal becomes an extension of themselves, with which they transcend ego and tap into their souls.

~ Anna Weber Literary Strategist,
MAOM Founder,
Voices in Print Publishing Successfully
Published Literary Strategies

CONTENTS

INTRODUCTION

There is no logical way to the discovery of these elemental laws. There is only the way of intuition, which is helped by a feeling for the order lying behind the appearance.

~ Albert Einstein

THIS IS ONE of the greatest times to be alive. There are so many choices you can make in your life. Access to the Internet has increased opportunities and, not only do you have instant access to nearly everyone you know through mobile phone calls and texting, you also have access to others all over the world through video chats.

Choices around relationship, career, finances, and health change continually and at times confusion abounds. Time appears to be moving quickly and solitary time seems to be a luxury of the past.

With so much stimulation and so many choices, what are you to do? How do you cope?

As a mental health therapist and intuitive coach, I have spent tens of thousands of hours with clients assisting them in making these decisions. As an intuitive mentor, I understand that you truly are the expert in your own life. Having a therapist or mentor can help you to clarify and stay focused on your goal and create the life you desire. Even with the luxury of one to one support, most of your growth happens between sessions. For years I have been tailoring Soul stems for clients to heal the issues they present and to assist them to stand firmly and unquestionably on their path to success.

So often fear has kept you from stepping into your vital, happy and confident Self. The Soul stems in this book will assist you in remembering who you truly are and transforming any resistance to living your highest vibration! You will be guided to use your intuition for empowered decision making.

In graduate school, the theorist I studied was Carl Jung. He gave us the understanding of the introvert and extrovert and also of the collective unconscious. He worked with archetypes, symbolism and dreams. Jung, Freud and other depth psychologists worked with complexes.

Beyond Freud's personal unconscious, Jung writes that there is a collective unconscious. In this writing process you are about to begin, you will access both. The collective unconscious is made up of universal knowledge that is common to all humans. You can access the collective unconscious through symbols that are found in dreams and myths and also through archetypes. You will be accessing these images through the psychic self-reading process in this book.

A complex is a collection of emotions, memories, images, ideas, and perceptions clustered around a common theme. They contribute to behaviors whether you are conscious of them or not.

In the process of developing intuition it is imperative that you unleash yourSelf from some of these complexes that tend to control your perception. Once free of these, you are able to get more accurate information. This is the incredible power of this journal process or as we therapists say "doing the work"!

An example of a complex is Addison, whose mother was a hoarder when Addison was young. Their home was not only disorganized, it was dirty and chaotic. They couldn't find anything. Even though as an adult she keeps a clean, organized home, she may have thoughts, emotions, and memories around this experience from childhood that fill her with shame and unworthiness today. This pattern in the psyche is a complex. These writing exercises will allow you to access and clear the energy that is stuck and free yourSelf from the complex.

In addition to the complex, there is the shadow side of an archetype or your personality. The shadow is the part that is in the dark, that you are not aware of; it can be the part you deny and relegate to the underworld. The shadow has power over you because it is hidden. When you bring it into the Light, into awareness, you can neutralize its power. This is one of the great benefits of this journal process.

Yes, you can use your own intuition to heal and live the outcome you desire. When you access your own inner wisdom you have the ability to bypass the ego. You can go beyond your conscious mind to your Higher Self, your Subconscious Self, your Intuitive Self - which allows you to **Live your Dreams Now!**

I have journaled for over 40 years and have found it to be one of the best tools to connect with my soul. It assisted me in syncing my inner life with my outer experiences and living a life of happiness, abundance, and joy!

Connecting to your soul has several benefits. Here are a few:

1. You begin to really know yourSelf.

2. What you believe and value and what you do become congruent.

3. You maximize your strengths.

4. The decision-making process becomes easier and more accurate.

5. You look inward for the truth rather than to other people's opinions.

6. You trust yourSelf.

7. You make empowering choices that lead to the next steps.

8. You may end up writing a book! ☺

How to Use this Book

There are two ways that you will activate your intuition with this book.

Firstly, I will teach you to use the same Intuitive Reading Process I use when I read my clients. After grounding and centering, you'll create a symbolic image that you will use as a Soul stem. If you prefer, you can use one of the Soul stems I have created for you.

Secondly, you will access your intuition through the Soul Stem's journal process. The more you journal, the better you will become at accessing your Intuitive Self. There have been times when I was writing and a part of me came through that I have never met before. It can be so amazing to experience the many facets of YOU!

Although not necessary, a great way to prepare yourSelf to receive an image is to use this simple grounding meditation I use daily. What I teach about grounding, the center of your head, neutrality, amusement, and running energy are all tools that came from my studies with the Church of Divine Man and the teachings of Mary Ellen Flora.

I suggest you bookmark the following page so you can return here prior to each section until you learn the meditation preparation by heart.

Grounding Meditation

Grounding is a self-healing tool. When you are grounded in present time you are able to manifest better. You cannot manifest when your body is in the future. To manifest, you create in your mind, but you need to make sure your body is grounded in present time.

Some people are more visual than others. If you can't visualize this, that's fine. Just say it to yourSelf and your body-mind will know what to do.

Your body feels safe when you are grounded. The energy that is released can be hurriedness, negative feelings, pain, or other people's energy that has attached to you. Releasing energy down the grounding cord can prevent stress, which may prevent illness.

After your meditation, take another deep breath from your belly and continue to release energy down your grounding cord.

It is important to practice this grounding as it will become more natural with practice.

Grounding Meditation Instructions

Close your eyes and take a deep breath from your belly. Pull your aura in around your body six to eight inches.

Choose a grounding cord like a waterfall, a beam of light, or a tree trunk. Imagine the grounding cord going down from the base of your spine below your tailbone down through the chair, the floor, and through the many layers of earth, all the way down into the fiery center of Mother Earth. Have the grounding cord be fully attached near the base of your spine and fully attached at the center of the Earth.

Starting at the top of your head, release energy from the top of your head all the way down your body and down your grounding cord.

The more you do this, the more you will sense the energy and the grounding.

Intuitive Reading Process

After you have done the grounding exercise – or, if you prefer, after you have taken a few deep breaths and relaxed - focus your attention in the center of your head. This is above and behind your eyes and between your ears. This is the place where you can look out with neutrality and amusement.

From the center of your head, imagine a white board about six to eight inches in front of your forehead. Later in this book I teach you to see a symbol related to what you are writing about. For instance, if you are in the section on Money, you may ask to see a symbol regarding a money issue.

As I close my eyes now, the image that comes to me is paper money fanned out. I see the symbols on the money changing from $1 to $100. I asked what that image means. The word that came was *fans*. That quickly translated to me to mean when I had more fans, I would increase my income. This is relevant to me today because a couple days ago I started practicing doing live stream videos on Periscope. The value of that is I would receive more Twitter followers and Periscope followers and be able to reach more people when I launch this very book!

The Soul stem that makes sense to me from the image is "If I had more Twitter fans . . ." That will be the next Soul stem I would write. There is an obvious thought about that, but the beauty of this process is that what comes up is so much more than what we can imagine.

When you get to the sections on the chakras, you'll see the information that is stored in each chakra. When you get an image that relates to that chakra, you will be able to see how the images can begin a process of deepening your writing experience and the information you receive.

If intuitively reading yourSelf is too overwhelming or you have difficulty with it, you don't have to worry. Just begin with the writing process and the Soul stems I provide. Whatever your Higher Self wants to share with you will come through, however you choose to use this book.

Soul Stems Journal Process

I am delighted to share with you the Soul Stem Journal Process. The best way to journal is to find a notebook or journal and a fast writing pen. There are two ways to use these stems. One is to just complete the sentences as fast as you can without thinking and write the answer to the questions one after another. The second way is to complete the stem in a journal, timing the writing for 10-20 minutes. When you are stuck just write "I don't know what to say" over and over until you become unstuck. This takes you deeper, underneath the surface thoughts. Start with 10 minutes and build up to 20 minutes. If you would prefer typing that's fine. They are both great tools and you can try each of them!

If you write in a notebook, I suggest you find a spiral notebook with holes or notebook paper. You may find that later on you want to put the pages in a 3-ring binder. I have over 30 years of journaling saved in binders and it is great to go back and look at what I've written. Of course, I don't keep the pages where I vented, but I do have some incredible experiences written down, like when the apparition of Black Elk came to me and shared a sacred teaching.

It is helpful to have a book to guide you and stir you on in your writing and in developing your intuition. Although I have journaled most of my life, it wasn't until I picked up Natalie Goldberg's *Writing Down the Bones: Freeing the Writer Within* that I was able to really validate myself as a writer and, even more, allow myself the luxury of taking time for myself to write. She was so honest about her creativity and how she wove her writing into all aspects of life. *Writing Down the Bones* gave this struggling single mom not only permission to take time to write, but also to value this introverted part of myself that fed me. Natalia Goldberg has been such an inspiration to me! Hopefully *Live Intuitively* will not only give you permission to take time for yourself, but also take a stand for your right to listen to yourself and use your intuition in your daily life.

When you are using the Soul stems, you may want to just open the book and choose a stem spontaneously. Focus on one at a time. If you want, you can use the same stem over and over again. If there is an area where you feel stuck, use one stem daily for a week. Notice how your writing changes.

You may notice that different voices surface. This is great. You can also begin to identify the different voices; different aspects of yourSelf. Remember, you are all the ages that you have ever been. Allow yourSelf to let these different ages come through.

Some of the Soul stems are repeated under different topics. This is to assist you in deepening your understanding of what is happening in that area of your life at that time.

Some of the Soul stems will have more of an impact on you than others and may be more difficult to journal. If you get stuck, keep at it. Showing up for the process will be worth it when you get to the other side!

Accountability Partner

Accountability is such a powerful motivator. People pay thousands of dollars a year to be accountable to show up and complete their goal or project.

In your case, an accountability partner is someone who you

can depend upon to assist you in your goals. You can share with your partner what you want to accomplish and check in with them to make sure that you did what you said you would do. If you are in a group that is teaching this book, by me or someone else, you may want to choose an accountability partner from the group. You can also find a partner in the online group I created for my students.

https://www.facebook.com/groups/
IntuitiveMastery/

What fun it would be to ask a friend to journal with you and share accountability. Start out writing and connecting daily to get a good sense of the process and then you can change to four to six days a week.

I remember when I was motivated to resume exercising and wanted to ride my recumbent bike for 30 minutes a day, I called my friend Cheyenne. I told her my plan to ride for 30 minutes a day for a week. I said that I would pay her $50 each day that I didn't ride. She said, "Great!" Did I pay her any money? Of course not! I rode to my heart's delight!

With students, I offer to be their accountability partner in this way: I assist them in setting their measurable goal. Then I ask them to write a check to the charity of their choice for the amount they want to invest. I keep the check and if *they do not follow through* and, at their direction, I mail the check to the charity.

Once you have journaled a few times, ask to join the Facebook group and introduce yourself!

https://www.facebook.com/groups/
IntuitiveMastery/

Share a summary with others of what you are learning from your writing experiences. You can make new friends and support each other as accountability partners.

This is an intuitive journal process, but I know many of you will also become published authors. Support each other!

PART ONE

"Don't try to comprehend with your mind.
Your minds are very limited. Use your intuition."

~ Madeleine L'Engle

BEGINNING SOUL STEMS

Time to Practice

YOU CAN CHOOSE specific areas in your life you would like to focus on. E.g. start from the beginning or choose one section at a time. For those of you who are highly organized, you may want to go from the beginning of the book to the end. Whatever you choose, you will definitely tap into your amazing Self!

Choose the Soul stem you want to journal in the area that you are focused on. Of course, you may not want to do all of them. You may wonder what Soul stem to choose. When I teach classes, I have my students look at the *Soul stem that scares them the most* and write that one!

Start this practice with at least one timed writing a day. Set a timer for 20 minutes or, if you prefer, use notebook paper or a three-ring binder and write for four full pages. If you can't write for 20 minutes, start with 10 minutes. You'll find that some Soul stems will activate a deeper part of you than others and you may write for longer. If you continually don't write for the 20 minutes, you may be blocked from allowing information to surface and I encourage you to push yourSelf a few times. Continue writing and let the deeper material surface.

Enjoy this powerful process of connecting to yourSelf and turning yourSelf inside out!

I'm really happy when . . .

What I like about myself . . .

I am SO tired of . . .

What I want to change is . . .

If they would listen, I would share . . .

Family

> ### *The capacity for friendship is God's way of apologizing for our families.*
>
> ~ *Jay McInerney*

Most of what you learn in life, you learn in your first six years. Your core experiences and beliefs come from your family - biological or inherited. Even though every family is significantly different than another, there are common experiences. Journaling about what has happened to you in the past - whether positive or negative - can enlighten you to who you are today and it can free up any blocks, so you can heal in the moment!

So often, clients come to my office stuck and frustrated. With this journal process you can shift and get some movement in your healing journey. You can transform and neutralize your painful stories so they no longer have an emotional charge.

Situations that used to put me in bed for days, I now view with compassion. I am forgiving of myself, as well as those who hurt me – whether that hurt was intentional or not. Bad memories are replaced with positive ones.

If your family memories are still too raw, then move to another section of this book and come back when you are ready. You can start with a Soul stem that will take you on a positive path. You understand by now though that, whatever Soul stem you choose, you will access the healing that is necessary for you now.

Some people easily fit in with their family like a puzzle piece. It is a beautiful experience. Others think the stork dropped them off at the wrong doorstep! Either way, your family members impact you in significant ways. Explore your relationship with your immediate and extended family:

What I learned from my father was . . .

What I learned from my mother was . . .

My favorite relative is . . .

I am so angry at my father when . . .

I am so angry at my mother when . . .

I am so angry at my [brother/sister/aunt/uncle/ grandparent, etc.] when . . .

What others don't know about my family is . . .

What I know about my family now is . . .

What supports me the most from my childhood is . . .

If only I could tell [family member] that . . .

The family secret that makes me sick is . . .

I cannot let go of the time that [family member] . . .

In order to heal, I need to forgive [name] for . . .

I need to forgive myself for . . .

What I love about my mother/father is . . .

What I love about my [family member] is . . .

Sometimes you are not able to communicate clearly or clear past issues with someone before they pass on. This was true of my relationship with my mother. We lost her suddenly when she was only 52 years old. There was so much that I would have liked to have said to her. I would have liked to have asked forgiveness for some of my attitudes and behaviors. In my book *12 Weeks to Self-Healing: Transforming Pain through Energy Medicine*, I wrote:

> **This book is dedicated to my mom,**
> **Shirley Jennie Topper.**
> **Had I known then what I know now ...**

You may have lost loved ones that you would like to complete with. Here are some Soul stems to assist you:

When I think of you, I . . .

What I regret now is . . .

If I had one more day with you I would . . .

What I didn't say to you is . . .

I am still angry with you about . . .

It really hurts when . . .

If you had only . . .

I wish I would have . . .

I could let you go if . . .

The gift you gave me is . . .

My memories of you . . .

I want to feel you in my heart, but . . .

I feel you around me when . . .

The family or environment you grew up in shaped your **beliefs and values**. Explore how you developed what you believe and how you live your life. Notice if you embraced the beliefs of your family or if you resisted and established your values apart from them.

Family should be about . . .

The greatest gift I got from growing up in my family is . . .

If I had a different upbringing, I would . . .

Everyday I think about the time when . . .

As an adult, you may choose a partner and create your own family. Your family may extend to new nieces, nephews and, later, grandchildren. Your connection to your family changes and healing may take place.

I love my [wife/husband] because . . .

I am so angry at my [wife/husband] because . . .

I love [child/grandchild] because . . .

I am so angry at [child/grandchild] because . . .

I am so angry at [niece/nephew/cousin] because . . .

The resentment I hold with my former wife is . . .

The resentment I hold with my former husband is . . .

I can improve my family relationships this year by . . .

What I need to complete with my family is . . .

I am happiest with my family when . . .

What I need to forgive myself for is . . .

What I have forgiven myself for is . . .

Friends

> *If you have two friends in your lifetime, you're lucky. If you have one good friend, you're more than lucky.*
>
> ~ S.E. Hinton

Some people are naturally able to make and keep friends and others struggle in this area of their lives. Jim Rohn said:

> **"You are the average of the five people you spend the most time with."**

In the case of friends, I think this is especially true. Whether you have friends you have known most of your life, or friends you feel you have known forever, there are still ups and downs in relationships. This section of the book will assist you in appreciating what you have in your friends, assess how you are as a friend, and may motivate you to make some changes with the friends you have.

The person who hurt me the most is . . .

I have no friends because . . .

Friends are important because . . .

My closest friend is . . .

The friend I've known the longest is . . .

When I do what I don't want to do I . . .

The person I most need to forgive is . . .

Being a Friend

These Soul stems will assist you in inventorying how you show up as a friend. There are times when you are able to be the friend that you want to be and other times when you let someone down. Perhaps, for some reason, you are afraid to make new friends. Perhaps you have so many friends that you are not able to be present to any of them in a heart-felt way.

I support my friends the most by . . .

I am a good friend when I . . .

I need forgiveness from . . .

I failed in my relationship with . . .

If I could do it over again, I would . . .

I would be a better friend if . . .

I hurt my friend . . .

I am not a very good friend because . . .

I am a great friend because . . .

The friend I judge the most is . . .

The friend I let down was . . .

As a friend, what I cannot do is . . .

Something I need to communicate to (name) is...

Receiving from your Friends

So often, I see that my clients have a difficult time receiving. Sometimes it's because they are so busy giving to others and other times it's that they neglect themselves. They seem to be batting away opportunities to receive one after another, without even recognizing it.

Friendships are ever changing. You may create new friends, let go of old friends, re-connect with previous friends, or stay connected throughout your whole life with a dear friend. There is an exchange of energy in friendships. With some you may find there is a good energy exchange and with others there could be an imbalance. It is helpful to explore how your friendships enhance your life and the life of your friends:

Friends are important because . . .

My closest friend is . . .

The friend I've had for the longest time is . . .

The friends I depend upon the most provide me with . . .

The friend who contributes the most to my life is . . .

I depend too much on . . .

I allow [name] to support me because . . .

I allow [name] to support me when . . .

The relationship that makes me feel powerful is . . .

I experience feeling worthy around . . .

Freedom is a value I experience when I am . . .

I have the most fun with . . .

My heart is so full of love when I am with . . .

To be my friend you have to . . .

I am most judged by . . .

The friend who criticizes me is . . .

The friend who betrayed me is . . .

When I was a child my best friend was . . .

What I loved about my childhood friend was . . .

The friend who supports my health is . . .

Qualities I choose in friends are . .

Challenges with Friends that may become Gifts

When I hear of challenges between friends who have once had a great connection before conflict hits hard, it reminds me of kittens. When kittens are young, they fight with each other and sometimes it appears they are going to really hurt each other. This practice prepares them for when there are real predators. It is the same with friendships. Some people did not have good role models to demonstrate to them how to be a friend or how to choose friends. Their pattern of relationship may be dysfunctional.

When communication is compromised and feelings are hurt, it may be an opportunity to learn about yourSelf and to deepen the friendship. You also may realize that your friend is simply not able to have a healthy friendship.

Just as kittens grow up and cats become independent and indifferent, you may find this with a friendship as well. Someone you once clicked with and shared deep secrets with may no longer be someone you want to spend time with.

At times you may realize that the friend, for some reason, has changed and you are no longer a good match. As difficult as it may be, there are times when it is important to allow yourSelf to stop being friends. This is especially important when you realize a friendship is toxic. These Soul stems will help you sort it out.

My closest friend is . . .

I am really drained by . . .

I feel guilty about my relationship with [name] because . . .

I need to forgive . . .

I need forgiveness from . . .

The person who hurt me the most is . . .

If I could do it over again, I would . . .

Friends are important because . . .

I am/was most hurt by . . .

The friend I neglect the most is . . .

The friendship I have had the longest is . . .

I am not a good friend to myself because . . .

I am no longer friends with . . .

The friend who is/was a detriment to my health is . . .

Before I die I need to . . .

Work and Career

I've learned that making a 'living' is not the same thing as 'making a life'.

~ Maya Angelou

Many people I have worked with looked at their life purpose as synonymous with their career. Yet our careers or the work we do is just a fraction of our purpose. We will explore this more in the chapter Exploring your Life Purpose.

In this section, let's look at the energy exchange you have between your work and your life force. Whatever it is you do for work - whether you are paid or not - there is an energy exchange. Too often, so much of your energy is given out and not replaced. This can leave you exhausted, depleted, and unhappy.

It is possible to either create the work you love or love the work you have. Let's explore this:

A strength I need to develop to be more successful is. . .

If I were willing to go for what I want, I would. . .

What challenges me about my work is . . .

What I love about my work is . . .

My ideal work would be . . .

I am reluctant to change . . .

I can't seem to change the fact that I . . .

I am most fearful when . . .

I am actually paralyzed when . . .

My resistance to work is . . .

If I only had [fill in the blank] I would . . .

If I only had [fill in the blank] I would be able to . . .

When I was young, I wanted to . . .

If I had the opportunity I could . . .

If money were no object I would . . .

Money would change me by . . .

Money would own me by . . .

I feel energized when I am . . .

I feel free when I am . . .

I am most stressed when . . .

I can contribute by . . .

Others think I am . . .

If I had more confidence I would . . .

In order to retire I need to . . .

I am a better employee when . . .

I am a better business owner when . . .

I am a better entrepreneur when . . .

I am successful when . . .

A fear I have about being successful is . . .

I will have peace of mind when . . .

What I love about my job is . . .

What I don't like about my job is . . .

I would be successful if . . .

What brings me happiness is . . .

To make the money I want I have to . . .

What I don't allow myself is . . .

I am confident that I can . . .

When unhappy I . . .

I am grateful for . . .

Many people see work as having social value - perhaps their friends are co-workers or business partners. Others create collaborative relationships to excel in their career or to make it more enjoyable. Explore how others affect your career:

The feedback I get from others is . . .

Contacting [name] would give me the ability to . . .

Contacting [name] would give me the opportunity to . . .

What others have that I don't is . . .

I am envious of . . .

I stand out from the others due to my . . .

The person who supports my work/career the most is . . .

The person who gets in my way is . . .

How I need to be supported is . . .

Coaching has helped me to . . .

Health

> *Be careful about reading health books.*
> *Some fine day you'll die of a misprint.*
>
> ~ *Markus Herz*

With a busy life, it is easy to neglect your health. Whether it be preventative care, medical appointments, or eating healthily and exercising, when you take time to journal, you become more conscious. Your body has a lot to say to you when you listen. With these Soul stems you can hear the whisper before it becomes a scream.

The energy of the choices that you make about your health are stored in the fifth chakra. In each of the Chakra sections of this book there is information and Soul stems pertaining to health in that chakra.

Just a couple of reminders – a good way to increase your health is to drink water all day long, add greens to your diet and just get up and move more!

This year I will improve my health by . . .

I get frustrated with myself when I continue to . . .

My health is so much better since I . . .

I have always been afraid of getting . . .

I take better care of my health when I am with . . .

I eat healthy when . . .

My worse eating habit is . . .

I know better but I still . . .

The friend who support my health is . . .

The friend who is a detriment to my health is . . .

The person who supports my health is . . .

The person who is a detriment to my health is . . .

I really need help with . . .

If I had support, I would . . .

My body screams to me . . .

The whisper I hear is . . .

The whisper I ignore is . . .

When I am elderly, I will . . .

I love my body by . . .

I am proud of myself when . . .

Grief

To weep is to make less the depth of grief.

~ William Shakespeare

Grief shows up for people in many different ways. What I have noticed is that, when there is a current loss, previous losses seem to attach to it. You can be overwhelmed by feelings, not only from the current loss, but also images and memories and feelings from the previous loss.

You may already be aware of *The 5 Stages of Grief*, written by Kubler-Ross. She shares that you go through these stages from one to the next and you can also go through all the stages in one day. The Stages are Denial, Anger, Bargaining, Depression, and Acceptance.

What you may notice about yourSelf most is the anger, bargaining, and depression. Anger is a secondary emotion - it covers up pain and fear. When you are feeling angry it may help to notice how you experience the anger in your body. I call it "running anger" because it feels like it is taking over your other senses. It is like you are running the energy of anger. It's helpful to journal about the underlying feelings of pain and fear, which I direct you into in the Soul stems.

You may notice the bargaining by hearing yourSelf say, "If I could have . . ." or "If only I had . . .". You search for ways that you could have changed the situation. Even though you may eventually notice you are depressed, it may be your friends and family who notice first. They may invite you to activities but you say you don't feel like it or don't have the energy.

When you are depressed, what you used to enjoy becomes bland to you. When you notice this, the anger has been "depressed" and it is critical that you allow yourSelf to feel your pain and identify your fear.

The Self-Help Toolbox on my website that is connected to my book *12 Weeks to Self-Healing: Transforming Pain through Energy Medicine* will provide you with several tools.

This Depression Assessment on this page will help you to assess whether you are depressed or not.

http://energymedicinedna.com/
self-help-toolbox/

Your anger also may show up as anxiety. The Anxiety Assessment Tool here will help you.

http://energymedicinedna.com/ self-help-toolbox/

The process of healing your grief is in these Soul stems. In fact, as I write this, I realized an old wound of my own has surfaced in order to heal. It has to do with feeling betrayed by a friend in the past. The trigger that brought this to my attention was a situation where I recently supported a current friend who was in conflict with another person. Although I didn't get in the middle, I had her back. The pain that came up for me was the realization that, in the previous situation, my friend did not have my back. At the time I was too hurt to talk with her about the situation. Now, I am journaling about it and when I can "take the charge" off, meaning getting to a neutral state, no longer feeling hurt or angry, then I can share with her.

In this section, I share some Soul stems for healing trauma as well. Past traumas can become stuck in the cells of your body and you can become frozen in your feelings and your memories. Feelings that are buried are buried alive and often surface when you don't want them too. They also surface when you feel somewhat safe, which means in your most precious relationships. Your journal is the perfect place for you to allow yourSelf to thaw out your feelings and heal the trauma. In my counseling practice, I have specialized in trauma for years. I highly suggest that, if you have deep trauma, to contact a counselor who is trained in EMDR - Eye Movement Desensitization Reprocessing.

http://www.emdr.com

This is the modality I have used with clients for many years to heal small traumas and major trauma such as: PTSD, childhood sexual abuse, rape, being robbed at gunpoint, and even torture. If you have a history of trauma, please reach out for help and allow yourSelf to receive healing.

The person I would love to see again is . . .

If only I could have said . . .

My heart was broken by . . .

I feel betrayed by . . .

I betrayed . . . I miss . . .

My lost opportunity was when . . .

What I love about [name] is . . .

What I miss about [name] is . . .

I can't tell her/him that . . .

I am so angry at . . .

I can barely move when I think of . . .

If only I had . . .

If I could do it over I would . . .

If only he/she would . . .

What scares me is . . .

If I stayed I would have . . .

I couldn't stay because . . .

It wasn't safe to . . .

I hurt him/her when I . . .

I am no longer interested in . . .

I am sad about . . .

I don't have the energy to . . .

I am discouraged about . . .

What irritates me is . . .

I wake up thinking about . . .

I can't get to sleep when . . .

My eating has changed by . . .

I can't decide . . .

I feel inadequate because . . .

My worth has plummeted since . . .

I am guilty of . . .

I am being punished for . . .

I am being punished by . . .

I feel powerless when . . .

I worry about . . .

The tension is . . .

I am edgy when . . .

Headaches happen when . . .

Fatigue causes . . .

I am exhausted because . . .

I am overwhelmed by . . .

I was traumatized by . . .

I have been supported by . . .

I set boundaries with . . .

My strength comes from . . .

I protect myself by . . .

I deserve . . .

I will receive . . .

Creativity

Imagination is everything. It is the preview of life's coming attractions.

~ Albert Einstein

Just the fact that you bought this book already tells me that you are creative! Creativity is a second chakra issue and there is more in that chapter you can write about as well.

Creativity can be like a three-edged sword. On one edge you have the clarity and the exhilaration of the process and the completed project. Another edge may be when your creativity is stuck and you engage in negative self-talk. You can also be overthinking - like you may be doing right now with the image of a three-edged sword! Really Candess? The third part of creativity that I struggle with is compulsive creating. My tendency is to create and create and create and I find myself overwhelmed with all my projects. If this is part of your process too, you may have stacks of notepads of what to create, unfinished projects and lists that would take a lifetime to finish.

I remember when I was a young girl, a third grader I believe, I was a Blue Bird. The next year I would transition into being a Camp Fire Girl. We recited the Blue Bird promises at each meeting. The only promise I remember is:

"I promise to finish what I begin."

Although not easy, it is a value that I attempt to keep up with.

Organization is critical to this task. One of my students shared with me an incredible free organizing tool. I have been able to organize my notes, stickies, and lists in one place online. My bulletin board is now one third the mess it once was and I am getting four times the work done. It was also instrumental in editing and making additions and changes to this book! The tool is called **Workflowy**. You get more space by referrals so be sure to connect with each other in the Facebook group to support each other and use each other's links!

https://workflowy.com/

A little note here: With the image of the three-edged sword. I taught you to use your Clairvoyance to see images. What is so incredibly fun about this is that images, like dreams, do not have to make any sense in themselves. They are projections that give meaning in your experience of them!

There are different ways to be creative. Some of us are artists and we flow like water through rooms, through projects, with friendships, and we continue in a creativity of color, textures, and images. Others, like myself, are more angular in our process and products and we tend toward being more like architects of a project. We revise and review several times before we release our masterpiece. This section will help you understand yourSelf more fully and assist you in being fully authentic in your creative process.

This year I will make time to . . .

I am so fulfilled and ecstatic when I . . .

Gratitude fills my heart when . . .

The most hair-brained idea I had was . . .

When I trusted my gut, I created . . .

I am not playful when . . .

Humor helps my creativity by . . .

I clear writer's block by . . .

I get burned out when . . .

What is meaningful is . . .

I enjoy teaching . . .

I can persuade others to . . .

I'm highly creative when . . .

I am a wizard when it comes to . . .

When I am insightful I . . .

I expand my ideas by . . .

I am competitive when . . .

I think out of the box about . . .

I am neurotic about . . .

I am my succinct best when . . .

The audience for my creative endeavors is . . .

My mental image of creativity is . . .

The truth about my creativity is . . .

I am excellent at . . .

My personality shows when I . . .

I smile at myself when . . .

Analyzing helps my creativity by . . .

I can't let my guard down by . . .

I am crazy enough to . . .

Consistency helps by . . .

I'm empathetic about . . .

I am best at storytelling when . . .

My rules of creativity include . . .

I will finish the project when . . .

I can expand my creative boundaries by . . .

My friends help me by . . .

A finished project is . . .

I can organize better by . . .

Abundance comes by . . .

Spirituality

> *We are all connected;*
> *To each other, biologically.*
> *To the earth, chemically.*
> *To the rest of the universe atomically.*
>
> ~ Neil deGrasse Tyson

In this section I want to be sensitive to your beliefs. I have chosen to use the word God/Goddess as a representative for the many names you may use such as: Jesus, the Divine, Universe, Creator, Source, etc. When you write out this sentence, please use your own word.

Spirituality means . . .

Spiritual people are able to . . .

What I believe about God/Goddess is . . .

If I could talk to God/Goddess I would ask . . .

I would be more kind if I . . .

I don't deserve because I . . .

If God/Goddess loved me I would . . .

If I could connect with God/Goddess, I would . . .

I should be punished because . . .

Hell is . . .

I believe angels . . .

When I die . . .

Heaven is . . .

I feel alone when . . .

My prayers are . . .

I can contact God/Goddess by . . .

God/Goddess only listens . . .

Church feels like . . .

When others don't believe . . .

When we think about God/Goddess and Heaven, we often think about our loved ones who have passed over. This section will give you some clarity on your beliefs. Remember that when you journal you are tapping into a part of yourSelf that is not always present to your conscious mind.

When I die I will . . .

[Name of loved one who has died] connects with me by . . .

What I believe about Heaven is . . .

What happens to people who die is . . .

Past lives means that . . .

When I die angels will . . .

The purpose I set up for this life was . . .

What confuses me the most is . . .

I wish I understood . . .

I wish I knew . . .

[Name of loved one who has died] please tell me . . .

My contribution in this lifetime has been . . .

What I need to complete before I die is . . .

Over the years I have helped clients and students to access their own guides. A guide may be one who has passed over such as a grandmother you loved, an angel, an archangel, or a spirit who has evolved to a higher level and comes to assist you.

When I was a student in a Healing Class at the Church of Divine Mind, we had an exercise where we connected to our healing guide. We went into meditation connected to our healing guide and received a name. The name I got was Kevin. Kevin – really Candess? Other students received cool names like Ariel and White Feather. I got Kevin!

The reality is we would not even be able to understand the actual name that guides have, but I could see that I needed a dose of humor and humility. Kevin was an incredible adjunct to my healing for many years. I called on Kevin to assist me when I placed hands on a friend's toe and healed a fracture and when I twisted my ankle stepping on a snowy path. Kevin has since left me. He taught me as much as was needed and in meditation I was given another healing guide – Moon Raven!

You may already have guides and not really know that they are your guides. Many people have Jesus, Quan Yin, St. Germaine, or Mother Mary. You will know in your heart if you have a deep connection with a guide!

I can't access a guide because . . .

I'm afraid of connecting with a guide . . .

If I believed in guides . . .

My guide helps me . . .

What I need from my guide is . . .

Why won't my guide . . .

What I have been taught about guides is . . .

My religion teaches . . .

I am so blessed by [guide name] when . . .

If I didn't listen to my guide . . .

My resistance keeps me from . . .

I am blessed when . . .

For most of my life I have been connected to and listening to my guides - way before I understood who they were or even that they were guides. I could write a whole book about my experiences, but I'll just share one.

Several years ago I was reading Sarah Ban Breathnach's book *Simple Abundance*. She wrote a daily page referencing the Harmonic Convergence. As I read the passage I started to tingle and had a big "ah-ha!" I realized that I was in Sedona during the Harmonic Convergence in August, 1987. This event was a special alignment of planets in our solar system and a powerful, synchronized meditation by those who resonated with this consciousness.

How I got there was, I awoke one morning and heard (in my mind) that I had to go to the Grand Canyon. *Really?* I thought. I'd never really traveled much and didn't understand why I was being directed there. I did, however, listen to messages that I got. I booked a flight and rented a car. At the airport the man at the car rental counter talked me into renting a Toyota 4Runner.

When I drove through Sedona I remember feeling like my

whole body was vibrating. Because of my sensitivity I didn't like the sensation at all - it was extremely uncomfortable. I continued to the Grand Canyon and it was beautiful. When I looked out over the canyon, I wondered why I was guided there. When I returned home, the only sense I could make of the trip other than the beauty I witnessed, was that I had a great time driving a 4Runner and I took lots of photos of it!

When I read the passage in the *Simple Abundance* book I clearly understood that my guides, who I now understand to be the Lords of Karma, had sent me to this monumental planetary shift so that my vibration would experience it and that the synchronized meditation would include the soul that I am. I realized in 1987 I was not conscious enough to be able to intellectually understand or connect with the Harmonic Convergence. I was able relate to the Grand Canyon.

I am so grateful for the guidance I have received from the Lords of Karma for most of my life. I now travel nationally and internationally assisting individuals and groups in raising the vibration of our beloved planet Earth.

Travel

> *The world is a book and those who do not travel*
> *read only one page.*
>
> *~ Augustine of Hippo*

Whether you experience travel by going to a nearby town, visiting your family in another state, or by exploring the world; travel expands your awareness. You can also explore traveling in your mind. With so many television channels today, you can go on an exploration of wildlife in Africa and visit Shakespeare and Co., a bookstore in Paris, all in the same day. You can almost taste the food when watching the foodie shows and can expand culturally on a tour of the Smithsonian with National Geographic. More recently, I have joined Periscope.com where I present Livestream videos while I travel. You can follow me and travel with me!

In this section you will become aware of hidden desires. Don't be surprised if you begin to remember a past life and have vivid images. If you don't believe in past lives, that's fine, just keep writing. Don't stop or judge what you write. Let whatever surfaces come through and allow yourSelf to be neutral about it or even amused.

This year I plan to travel . . .

I can't travel because . . .

I really want to see . . .

My favorite trip was . . .

Traveling means . . .

If I could, I would go . . .

Traveling is fun with . . .

I am stressed when . . .

I can't afford to . . .

I am saving to . . .

An all expense-paid trip would be to . . .

I am most connected to [place] . . .

I dream of . . .

I would never want to go to . . .

I am scared when . . .

My greatest fear is . . .

When traveling, what if . . .

I am intrigued by . . .

The culture I enjoy is . . .

The culture I am turned off by is . . .

In a past life I lived in . . .

In a past life I lived as . . .

The books I read are set in . . .

The time period that excites me is . . .

My curiosity is about . . .

Alone, I would never . . .

Traveling in groups is . . .

Traveling alone is . . .

My commitment to mySelf is to . . .

Play

> *This is the real secret of life - to be completely engaged with what you are doing in the here and now. And instead of calling it work, realize it is play.*
>
> *~ Alan W. Watts*

The word "play" conjures up colorful images! I see people on the Amazing Race, an American television show where they race all around the world almost like on a scavenger hunt and they look like they are having a blast! For me, this would be exhausting and anything but fun. Some people love driving race cars or Four-Wheelers. Other people's idea of fun is lying in the sun with a suspense or romance novel. There are so many ways to come alive and live passionately!

With clients, I assist them in bringing balance into their lives. When we talk about what they do to play, too often the response is they don't know how play. They seem lost.

At a dinner party recently a woman and I were talking about journaling. She said she once took a writing class and the instructor gave her the assignment to journal about play. She said she dropped out of the class because she couldn't figure out how she plays. This became a hot topic at the table. When questioning her I found out that she enjoys gardening and reading. The conversation resulted in several people understanding that they imagined play as something active such as roller-skating or bungee jumping. She realized that gardening, reading and watching movies was her play!

The reality is that play is different for everyone. For those who are introverted, play often involves activities that are quiet and peaceful. Hiking, sitting near a stream, quilting, or even shopping can be play.

Then again, some people can barely stop playing to show up for work and family. Their whole life is about having fun and most of their friends are active too. The continuum of play goes on and on. Most of us end up somewhere in the middle.

How you express your play and your passion may crossover. Let's see what you find out about yourSelf:

Play for me is . . .

I am most alive when I . . .

I can play when . . .

I laugh the most when . . .

My playmates are . . .

I can't have fun when . . .

When I was a child I played by . . .

I feel out of control when . . .

I get an adrenaline rush when . . .

My friends say I . . .

My spouse/kids say I . . .

I am reluctant to . . .

You can't stop me from . . .

If I had two weeks off from work I would . . .

If I were retired I would . . .

The last time I played hard was . . .

The best play is . . .

[Name] and I play . . .

If I had the energy I would . . .

I am going to allow myself to . . .

I am grateful for . . .

I am passionate about . . .

Passion means . . .

PART TWO

Intuition is seeing with the soul.

~ Dean Koontz

EXPLORING THE CHAKRAS

YOU MAY WANT to go back to How to Use this Book (where I suggested you place a bookmark) to review the process of preparing to read yourSelf.

This is especially important when reading your chakras.

CHAKRA ONE

*You are truly home only
when you find your tribe.*
~ Srividya Srinivasan

THE FIRST CHAKRA is the Root Chakra, which relates to instinct, being in a physical body, safety, security, the ability to stand up for oneself, tribal information, and potential in the material world. Health issues related to the root chakra involve the immune system, coccyx, anus, large intestine, adrenal glands, back, legs, feet, and bones. The major issue is survival and having a right to be here.

When you are looking at your chakra psychically, here are some images you may see that represent the first chakra:

- *Inability to stand* – may represent not being able to stand up for yourSelf, stand up to someone else, get back on your feet, needing to rest.

- *Kittens fighting* – may represent learning to protect yourSelf, sharpening your skills, discord with a sibling, safely bantering to grow.

- *Being apart from a group* – may represent isolating yourSelf, not fitting in, being a voyeur.

NOTE: Some of the information on chakras comes from the work of Caroline Myss. I have attended her workshops and taught from her books for many years.

Family

The foundation you are given as a child sets the stage for your entire life. As I stated earlier in the book, you learn more in the first six years of your life than you learn in the rest of your life.

I grew up in a dysfunctional family, which made it difficult for me to fit in socially. Due to depression, I ended up in the office of a psychiatrist. When he was talking to me about my family and how they influenced me, I remember how adamantly I defended how children are affected by friends, neighbors, teachers, television and everything else I could muster up. As an independent soul, I was not willing to own being like my mother - who I later understood I judged as a victim or damsel. I adored my father and was protective of him. I didn't want to see that my angry outbursts were learned from him. Later, of course, I understood that whether we "don't fall far from the tree" or resist and behave in the opposite of our loved ones, our family shapes how we experience the world. Here are some soul seeds to help you decide for yourSelf.

My parents still believe . . .

What I want to teach my children is . . .

What still hurts from childhood is . . .

The difficulty with my mother is . . .

I appreciate my mom when . . .

The difficulty with my father is . . .

I appreciate my dad when . . .

My dad's voice in my head says . . .

The dad I wanted would have . . .

My mom's voice in my head says . . .

The mom I wanted would have . . .

What I really think is . . .

The memory that haunts me from childhood is . . .

Who I have yet to forgive from my childhood is . . .

I still blame my family for . . .

If my childhood had been different, I would be . . .

My family blessed me with . . .

I bless my children with . . .

Rituals I continue from childhood are . . .

Tribal Information

The first chakra contains information about your tribe. In addition to your family, you have other tribes with which you belong. As a young person, your classmates or friends were your tribe. If you were involved in activities in school, your teammates or the other musicians or singers were your tribe. Other tribes you are connected with may be religious or cultural. You may belong to a tribe of authors, quilters, politicians, entrepreneurs, or young moms. I love the city of Spokane where I live and people who live here are members my tribe. Everyone in my neighborhood by the river is a member of my eclectic tribe.

Whatever tribe you belong to, you often - knowingly or not - align with their beliefs and values. When I was younger I entered into a relationship with a man who was abusive. In the cycle of abuse, I was scared and not sure what to do. This was in the mid 1970s and my way out was to join the tribe of the women's movement. I joined NOW, the National Organization of Women. As a young single mom, this powerful movement was what I needed to break out of that relationship and away from the man who, although alcoholic and abusive, was my soul mate.

Caroline Myss teaches extensively about tribes relating to the first chakra. In her book *Anatomy of the Spirit*, she says that when we are in a tribe we move at the same pace as that tribe. That is an interesting concept. When I think of that I think about the Catholic church which in some ways moves at a snails pace. Then I look at Social Network tribes (Facebook, Twitter, Instagram, Periscope, etc.) which move instantaneously.

You can gleam a lot of insight by recognizing the tribes to which you belong:

Traditions that are important to me are. . .

I need others most when . . .

The tribe [group] I am supported by is . . .

What I really think about my tribe is . . .

I am superstitious about . . .

Who I have yet to forgive from my childhood is . . .

If my childhood had been different, I would be . . .

Rituals I continue from childhood are . . .

Tribal information that still affects me is . . .

The rules that hold me back . . .

My tribe holds me back by . . .

I no longer fit into my tribe because . . .

The tribe I've given up is . . .

The tribe I'd like to join is . . .

I was hurt by . . .

I was rejected by . . .

My life will change when . . .

Safety and Survival

Children who grow up in unstable or dysfunctional homes may have a high need for safety when they are older. Even if you had a secure childhood, you may be highly sensitive, which will cause you to feel/sense more than others do. Your high need for safety may result in your having negative reactions when you are frightened. As a child you probably comforted yourSelf with a favorite blanket or teddy bear for a longer period than most children. As an adult you become overwhelmed easily and retreat. You are highly aware, maybe even hypervigilant, and automatically on guard.

Here are some signs of those who grew up in homes where they felt unsafe:

- Tendency to be highly organized and plan ahead to offset any unexpected changes.

- Disassociation – separating from your body - which allows you detach from reality.

- Numbing through use of food, alcohol or other drugs, or process addictions such as shopping, gaming, or gambling.

- Avoid looking at your issues.

- Behave defensively.

- Have difficulty telling the truth.

- Align with religious groups to feel safe.

Working with these Soul stems can be scary for you if you don't feel safe. It is helpful to find a group or a partner that you can share with. This is the opportunity to heal and, when you do it with others, you begin to normalize your experiences and realize you are not alone. Whichever way you choose to work, you can empower yourSelf by activating your intuition with this process.

You can find more information about one of my reactive situations in *The Queen Archetype* I wrote for *Live Encounters Magazine*.

http://energymedicinedna.com/the-queen-archetype-2/

A more recent reaction was when I was in Venice in 2015. It was late when we checked into the room my friend had booked through Airbnb.com. I walked into the room and there was a bed that had a wooden clothes rack on top of it and other people's clothes were drying on it. The room did not seem clean to me and there was no bathroom attached. I immediately reacted and was angry with my roommate for not discussing with me what my needs were regarding a room. I guess I slept there that night, but I don't remember. Must be the dissociation.

The next day, as we ventured out for our journey in Venice, right by where we stayed was a hotel with a patio looking out at the water and a man sitting there with his MacBook Pro. I knew immediately, that was where I wanted to stay. I talked with the hotel clerk and negotiated a deal since we were already paying for another place in Venice. It was a delightful room, small but perfect, and with a view of the lagoon. The morning breakfast was full of delicious foods including croissants, yogurt, eggs, sweets, and great coffee, in contrast to packaged sugary bread, and instant coffee in the BnB!

As delighted and full of gratitude that I was to be in Venice - which is my heart place - when old triggers surface, they surface.

As a child I spent a lot of time in my bedroom to avoid the chaos of the rest of the house. I see now that where I sleep is important because of this. I comforted myself with books and writing. As a young adult, journaling became a sacred way of connecting with mySelf and I loved it. Today my journal is an extension of mySelf. With it, I transcend my ego and tap into my Soul!

I compromised myself when I ...

What I am afraid to say is ...

What I am afraid to write is ...

What comforts me the most is ...

The person I have compromised most with is ...

Who I have yet to forgive from my childhood is ...

What my child self wants to do more of is ...

I overreacted when ...

When I feel unsafe I ...

My high need for safety created ...

When [name] is impatient with me ...

I still blame my family for ...

My family blessed me with ...

If I felt safe, I would ...

I'd like to feel safe when ...

Values

The simple values of childhood become complicated as you experience life. The black and white clarity of right and wrong becomes gray. You begin to understand "situational ethics" and your beliefs and choices begin to align you with some people and alienate you from others. Some basic values are honesty, integrity, compassion, loyalty, ethics, respect, sharing, and truth. This section will allow you to review your values from childhood and become clear on what you believe and what you value in your life today.

What I thought was important when I was 10 was . . .

What I want to teach my children is . . .

The strangest superstition I have is . . .

What I value most is . . .

I would never . . .

I compromised myself when I . . .

I was so embarrassed when . . .

The memory that haunts me from childhood is . . .

Three words that describe my code of honor are . . .

The part of me I have compromised the most is my . . .

I am still so angry at . . .

What I value most from my childhood is . . .

What my child self wants to do more of is . . .

I still blame my family for . . .

My family blessed me with . . .

I bless my children with . . .

The most powerful choice I have made is . . .

I am most honest with . . .

The reason I tell lies is . . .

I lie the most to [name] because . . .

If I were truthful . . .

When I lie I feel . . .

When I am truthful I feel ...

What integrity means is ...

My incongruence affects my integrity by ...

People who say one thing and do another ...

I don't keep my word when ...

When I don't keep my word, I ...

Compassion keeps me from ...

Compassion supports my character by ...

I am most compassionate when ...

I don't feel any compassion for ...

Ethically, I cross the line when ...

What ethics mean to me is ...

Ethics don't concern me because ...

Other people's ethics bother me when ...

I am most loyal to ...

[Name]'s loyalty to me is ...

If I were loyal, I would not have ...

If I were loyal, I would ...

I ended a friendship because ...

My respect for myself is ...

I don't respect ...

I don't respect people who ...

To earn my respect you have to ...

I lost respect for [name] when ...

[Name] does not respect me by ...

I would give respect if . . .

I share easily with [name] because . . .

I am don't share with [name] because . . .

I feel guilty for not sharing my . . .

[Name] expects me to share . . .

The truth is . . .

I don't believe when you say . . .

I don't tell the truth because . . .

It's important to tell the truth when . . .

Health

The chakras are like little energy centers of vital information. The issues related to your health are included in your chakra. Caroline Myss says "your biography is your biology." This means that what happens in your emotional life ends up in your physical body. You'll find some emotional Soul stems that are significant to your health in this section.

To intuitively read your health, do the **Grounding Meditation** that you bookmarked earlier. Before the Intuitive Reading Process, you will also want to do a Body Scan:

BODY SCAN INSTRUCTIONS

Close your eyes, take a deep breath, ground, and focus on your body - beginning at the top of your head.

Just scan your body downward, being aware of any tension, unusual sensation, or any place that you feel stuck energy, discomfort, or pain. Just notice this.

Then continue to the Intuitive Reading Process. Ask for a symbol related to your health.

Health issues that may arise from first chakra imbalances:

- Immune related disorders
- Adrenal insufficiency (fatigue)
- Frequent illness
- Eating Disorders such as obesity, anorexia, and malnourishment
- Disorders of the bones and teeth, osteoporosis
- Disorders of the bowel, anus, and/or large intestine, such as rectal tumors and cancer
- Problems with the legs, including varicose veins
- Lower back pain and sciatica
- Problems with the base of the spine, buttocks, legs, knees and feet

When I am healthy, I . . .

My energy wanes when . . .

I am sick of . . .

When I am grounded . . .

I'm afraid to be in my body because . . .

I overeat when . . .

I can't seem to eat because . . .

My digestion is . . .

I don't take a stand when . . .

I am depressed about . . .

I am anxious when . . .

The pain in my [name place in your body] is due to . . .

I don't get off my feet because . . .

I don't rest when . . .

If I rest . . .

Taking better care of my self would mean . . .

I could take better care of my health by . . .

I punish myself by . . .

If I loved myself, I would . . .

Affirmations for the First Chakra

- I am safe and grounded.
- I have a right to be here.
- I love my body.

- I deserve and receive nurturing.
- I live abundantly.
- I am happy, healthy and joyful.

There is more information on Chakra One on my website, including information on how to balance your First Chakra:

http://energymedicinedna.com/chakra-one

CHAKRA TWO

*Indifference and neglect often do much more damage
than outright dislike.*

~ J.K. Rowling

THE SECOND CHAKRA is the Sacral Chakra which relates to relationship, emotions, intimacy, sexuality, creativity, work, and money. It is associated with sensual movement and with sexuality. Health issues related to the sacral chakra involve hips, lower back, reproductive organs, prostrate, bladder, kidneys, stomach, large intestine, pelvis, appendix, and bodily fluids. The major issues of the second chakra are movement, connection, and pleasure.

When you are looking at your chakra psychically, here are some images you may see that represent the second chakra:

- *Book or creative project* – may represent needing to complete the project, being in process, or a book you need to write to tell your story.

- *Rotting peach or other fruit* – may represent not being fruitful, withholding love and decaying, losing life energy.

- *Money flowing in a whirlwind* – inability to grasp your abundance, money being outside your grasp, financial fear.

Sexuality and Intimacy

Sexuality is a part of who you are. Your values and behaviors around your sexuality are very personal. Intimacy is one way in which you connect with others and can deepen your relationship.

If you have a history of sexual abuse, this may be a difficult section for you and I encourage you to journal with a friend or have a counselor with whom you can share. Do not be surprised if memories surface for the first time. As a counselor, I have successfully assisted clients in healing from childhood sexual abuse for over 25 years.

In addition to journaling as a tool for self-care, the modality I use - which is the most effective I know of - is EMDR (Eye Movement Desensitization Reprocessing.) You can find more information and a therapist to help you on their website.

https://www.emdr.com

A powerful choice I made is . . .

The scariest choice I made is . . .

I compromise myself when I need . . .

I feel most powerful when . . .

It is totally unethical to . . .

I need to call my Spirit back from . . .

The person I control most is . . .

The person who controls me most is . . .

A sexual woman is . . .

A sexual man is . . .

My sexuality feels . . .

I feel seductive when . . .

I prostitute myself when . . .

The abuse I can't release is . . .

The secret I keep is . . .

When I can't feel, I . . .

I was abused by . . .

I abused . . .

I was hurt by . . .

I hurt . . .

I don't want to feel . . .

If I were free from these memories . . .

I am pleasured by . . .

When I move my body, I . . .

I desire . . .

I am needy when . . .

I am seduced by . . .

I seduce . . .

What I love about my sexuality is . . .

I feel sexy when . . .

I love to move to . . .

The sensations I enjoy are . . .

Relationships and Emotions

The first relationships you will experience are with your family or care givers. Also, you will learn about yourSelf by being with your friends and in relationships with classmates and neighbors. By the time you are an adult, your experiences and your environment have shaped you. What you believe and the choices that you make regarding relationships continue to change. Life situations may become imprinted and at times you'll react rather than respond.

This section will take you deeper into surveying your relationships and your emotional responses. Using your intuition in this section will awaken you to identifying your past intuitive hits and help you to be able to isolate those hits in the future and make the best intuitive decisions.

The powerful choice I made is ...

The scariest choice I made is ...

I compromise myself when I need ...

I feel most powerful when ...

It is totally unethical to ...

I need to call my Spirit back from ...

The person I control most is ...

The person who controls me most is ...

The relationship that empowers me most is ...

The relationship where I lose the most power is ...

I am enmeshed with ...

I was enmeshed with ...

I cross boundaries with ...

I have crossed boundaries with ...

My boundaries are being crossed by ...

I was betrayed by ...

I am safe with ...

I forgive ...

I will never forgive ...

I was unfaithful to ...

When [name] cheated on me ...

I pretend I'm satisfied with ...

I convinced myself that ...

I should feel lucky about ...

I'm not thriving when ...

I support those I love by ...

This section may bring up some thoughts that would lead you to the Family and Friends section in in Part One.

Creativity

Creativity has been addressed in detail in Part One. Here I am repeating the Soul stems for activating your Creativity.

This year I will make time to . . .

I am so fulfilled and ecstatic when I . . .

Gratitude fills my heart when . . .

The most hair-brained idea I had was . . .

When I trusted my gut, I created . . .

I am not playful when . . .

Humor helps my creativity by . . .

I clear writer's block by . . .

I get burned out when . . .

What is meaningful is . . .

I enjoy teaching . . .

I can persuade others to . . .

I'm highly creative when . . .

I am a wizard when it comes to . . .

When I am insightful I . . .

I expand my ideas by . . .

I am competitive when . . .

I think out of the box about . . .

I am neurotic about . . .

I am my succinct best when . . .

The audience for my creative endeavors is . . .

My mental image of creativity is . . .

The truth about my creativity is . . .

I am excellent at . . .

My personality shows when I . . .

I smile at myself when . . .

Analyzing helps my creativity by . . .

I can't let my guard down by . . .

I am crazy enough to . . .

Consistency helps by . . .

I'm empathetic about . . .

I am best at storytelling when . . .

My rules of creativity include . . .

I will finish the project when . . .

My resistance keeps me from . . .

I can expand my creative boundaries by . . .

My friends help me by . . .

A finished project is . . .

I can organize better by . . .

Abundance comes by . . .

Money

Money, money, money! There are so many views about money. There is the "love of money," "money is evil," "rich people are selfish," and "poor people are lazy." Attitudes about money go on and on.

This section guides you to understand how *you* feel about money and how it affects your life and your health. Manifesting is often taught in two ways. One is to be exact and detailed about what you want to manifest. Another, which is what I currently teach, is to focus on feeling how you will feel when you have what you desire and don't limit the way in which you receive it.

In either case, often right after you start your process, there is a voice that pops up saying things like: "you can't do this," "this won't work for you," or "you are not worthy, deserving." I ask students to slow their mind down in order to be able to catch these thoughts. Often they go by without conscious awareness. When they are able to grab them, I have them write them down and then challenge them. "Why not me! Yes, I am worthy and I can manifest ..."

After you get an intuitive symbol and write out the Soul stems, be sure to go back in your journal and circle the areas where you need to challenge any negative beliefs that come up for you.

A powerful choice I made is . . .

The scariest choice I made is . . .

I compromise myself when I need . . .

I feel most powerful when . . .

It is totally unethical to . . .

I need to call my Spirit back from . . .

When I have money I feel . . .

When I have no money I feel . . .

When I have outstanding bills I . . .

When I spend lots of money, I feel . . .

Rich people are . . .

Poverty is a sign of . . .

If I had a million/billion dollars to spend immediately, I would . . .

Charity means . . .

The person I have to be financially accountable to says . . .

I waste money by . . .

I save money because . . .

When I hide money I feel . . .

What I envision buying with money is . . .

Work

When I think about work, one of the most important aspects is the energy exchange. Some people love their job and are energized by it. Others show up, do what they have to do, and leave emotionally exhausted.

How you think about your work makes the difference. When I was in my late teens and a single mother, I worked at a local nursing home mopping floors. I enjoyed it. It was easy work and I loved talking to the elderly patients there. Now I have my own business and, although I am really busy, I love teaching, coaching and mentoring, and reading and healing clients. When I encounter something I don't like in my work, I either don't do it, or I change my attitude.

These Soul stems will help you identify where you naturally thrive and where you need to make changes, either in your job or your attitude.

My tendency to underachieve/overachieve . . .

I am energized by . . .

I am drained when . . .

To prepare for creativity, I . . .

My coworkers . . .

When I take breaks . . .

If I were my own boss . . .

I contribute by . . .

If I changed jobs I would . . .

I am grateful for . . .

The attitude that needs changing is my . . .

The powerful choice I made is . . .

The scariest choice I made is . . .

I compromise myself when I need . . .

I feel most powerful when . . .

It is totally unethical to . . .

I need to call my Spirit back from . . .

Health

The chakras are like little energy centers of vital information. The issues related to your health are included in your chakras. Caroline Myss says "your biography is your biology." This means that what happens in your emotional life ends up in your physical body. I share more about this in the Fifth Chakra. I've included some emotional Soul stems that are significant to your health in this section.

To intuitively read your health, do the **Grounding Meditation** that you bookmarked. Before the Intuitive Reading Process, you will also want to do a Body Scan.

BODY SCAN INSTRUCTIONS

Close your eyes, take a deep breath, ground, and focus on your body beginning at the top of your head.

Just scan your body downward being aware of any tension, unusual sensation or any place that you feel stuck energy, discomfort or pain. Just notice this.

Then continue to the Intuitive Reading Process. Ask for a symbol related to your health.

Health issues that may arise from second chakra imbalances.

- Health issues related to the reproductive organs
- Fibroids, endometriosis, pelvic inflammation
- Prostate problems, prostate cancer
- Disorders of the spleen and urinary system
- Bowel disease, colitis, Crohn's, Irritable bowel syndrome
- Menstrual difficulties, PMS PMDD

- Sexual dysfunction, frigidity, impotence, sexual addiction
- Chronic lower back pain, sciatica
- Inflexibility of joints
- Loss of sensual pleasure (food, sex, other interests)

What creates the tension in my body is . . .

When I deny myself pleasure, I . . .

Rigid boundaries cause me to . . .

I need to set boundaries with . . .

When I resist change, I . . .

If I were to allow myself to be loved, I . . .

My frigidity hurts me by . . .

Promiscuity leaves me feeling . . .

Inflexibility shows up in my body as . . .

My back hurts when I . . .

The person I carry on my shoulders is . . .

I eat to cover pain from . . .

I am afraid to feel my feelings because . . .

My drinking (drug use) scares me when . . .

After over-eating, I feel . . .

What I can't stomach anymore is . . .

I just can't digest (situation) . . .

If I listened to my body, I would . . .

Today I will love myself by . . .

Affirmations for the Second Chakra

- My feelings guide my intuition.
- I deserve an abundance of pleasure.
- I move easily and effortlessly.
- I am a sacred, healthy, sexual [woman/man].
- I live abundantly.
- I am happy, healthy and joyful.

There is more information on Chakra Two on my website, including information on how to balance your Second Chakra.

http://energymedicinedna.com/chakra-two

CHAKRA THREE

*This life is yours. Take the power to choose what
you want to do and do it well. Take the power to
love what you want in life and love it honestly.
Take the power to walk in the forest and be a part
of nature. Take the power to control your own life.
No one else can do it for you. Take the power to
make your life happy.*

~ *Susan Polis Schutz*

THE THIRD CHAKRA is the Solar Chakra, which relates to vitality, energy distribution, inner strength, self-control, power, ego, self-expression, personality, desire, care of self and others, and self-esteem. Health issues related to the solar chakra involve the digestive system, stomach, liver, pancreas, gall bladder, spleen, and adrenal glands. The major issues of the third chakra are power and individualization.

Many of us are aware of the third chakra because we are often aware of the "gut feelings" we get. As you develop your intuition you will notice this even more. When I read clients, the third and the fifth chakras are the ones that usually need the most clearing.

When you are looking at your chakra psychically, here are some images you may see that represent the third chakra:

- *Being hit in the gut* – may represent losing power, being disabled, being hurt or betrayed by a loved one.

- *Water down a drain* – may represent energy going down the drain, money down the drain, or an energy leak in your health.

- *Body of water* – may represent emotions and the emotion will depend on whether the water is stagnant, flowing downhill, or leaking slowly.

Vitality

So often you are affected energetically by your environment. This includes where you live, your home environment, the colors around you, and the people you spend time with. You are also strongly affected by what you eat. The fact that you are reading this book means that you are most likely more sensitive than others.

When writing about vitality, you may begin to notice a pattern of how your energy changes.

In my private practice I often teach clients how to protect themselves energetically. First do the grounding meditation you used to prepare for reading your chakras in the How to Use this Book section. You can imagine a Golden, White Light coming down from the heavens, through the top of your head and filling up your body and energy field six to eight inches around your body. Feel the powerful, protective energy. Then outside the Golden, White Light, surround yourself with violet light. You can image this or just ask that it happen for you. This will protect you.

Another protective tool comes from Donna Eden. This Zip Up Tool will protect you from having other people hit you energetically. They often do this without even knowing it with their words or how they look at you.

THE ZIP UP TOOL

Imagine you are zipping up a jacket from the bottom of the jacket, up to right under your lower lip.

Once you bring your hand up the imaginary jacket to your lower lip, turn your fingers as if you were locking it. Do this three times.

Next put your hand at the back of your neck (where a hood would attach) and bring it over the top of your head to right above your top lip. Lock it. Do this three times.

This is a great tool I use whenever I go out and especially when I am in a mall or hospital. You can pair this with eating. After each meal, zip up and go.

You can find my 12 Minute Energy Healing Meditation on my website.

http://energymedicinedna.com/ 12-minute-energy-clearing-meditation

I am energized by . . .

I come alive when . . .

I am deflated when . . .

I was hit in the gut by . . .

I need approval from . . .

The person I don't like but spend time with is . . .

I have resentments against . . .

My energy is drained by . . .

I give my power away when . . .

I give my power away to . . .

I gain power when I . . .

If I had more energy . . .

I feel most vital when . . .

Strength, Self-control, Self-expression, Self-esteem, and Power

When you notice where your energy goes, you can make empowering choices in your life. Keeping your energy and focusing in present time assists you in manifesting what you desire.

There is a fine balance between being empowered and expressing yourself, and attempting to control how others express themselves.

There is a lot to learn from the third chakra and it can be so empowering and freeing!

What my gut tells me is . . .

What I know to be true is . . .

What I like about myself is . . .

I wish my life were more . . .

I wish my life were less . . .

I don't stick to my commitments when . . .

I know I should . . .

I can't seem to continue to . . .

I know I shouldn't . . .

I avoid responsibility by . . .

What I don't like about myself is . . .

What I want to change about myself is . . .

What I will change about myself is . . .

I'm critical when it comes to . . .

I protect myself by . . .

The person I blame the most is . . .

The person who give me feedback about myself is . . .

I accept feedback from . . .

I am defensive around . . .

I am afraid of . . .

I learn from . . .

What others don't understand about me is . . .

Others are critical of me about . . .

What my gut tells me is . . .

What I know to be true is . . .

Care of Self and Care of Others

In over 30 years of counseling clients, the biggest issue I have seen is people's unwillingness to take the time for self-care. It appears that, in their desire to connect with others, they neglect themselves. Naturally they become depleted and angry with those who do not do what they want. They feel angry and then act out of control. The greatest way to be in control (which is impossible actually) is to focus on getting your own needs met and giving to others out of your excess and not your need.

One of the greatest gifts you can give to yourSelf is to allow yourSelf to receive. If you spend one week noticing what others offered you and you turned down, you would see the pattern that you have created. When I listen to clients, so often the image I see is of them batting away all the help others are offering. This can be a self-esteem issue.

In addition to noticing what you don't receive, you may even want to ask others for help. A great exercise is to ask three people for help in one week. Notice how you feel when you do this. If fear surfaces, jot down in your journal what you say to yourSelf. These Soul stems will clarify your care of self and others.

My gut tells me . . .

What I know to be true is . . .

I know I should . . .

I can't seem to continue to . . .

I know I shouldn't . . .

I avoid responsibility by . . .

What I don't like about myself is . . .

What I want to change about myself is . . .

What I will change about myself is . . .

I'm critical when it comes to . . .

I protect myself by . . .

The person I blame the most is . . .

The person who gives me feedback about myself is . . .

I accept feedback from . . .

I am defensive around . . .

I learn from . . .

What others don't understand about me is . . .

Others are critical of me about . . .

I feel responsible for . . .

I feel responsible to . . .

I wish my life were more . . .

I wish my life were less . . .

What my gut tells me is . . .

What I know to be true is . . .

Ego/Personality

The concept of the ego comes from Freud's construct of the id, ego and superego. The ego, which is the self, is said to mediate between the id and the superego. In a great simplification, the id is the instinctual impulsive part of you and the superego is the perfectionistic part that identifies and follows rules.

Wikipedia states from Ruth Snowden's *Teach YourSelf Freud*

> *The ego is the organized part of the personality structure that includes defensive, perceptual, intellectual-cognitive, and executive functions. Conscious awareness resides in the ego, although not all of the operations of the ego are conscious.*

> *Originally, Freud used the word ego to mean a sense of self, but later revised it to mean a set of psychic functions such as judgment, tolerance, reality testing, control, planning, defense, synthesis of information, intellectual functioning, and memory. The ego separates out what is real. It helps us to organize our thoughts and make sense of them and the world around us.*

Author and medical intuitive Caroline Myss says

> *The soul in us is a vessel drawn to goodness. The ego is a vessel drawn to darkness, and therein lies our battle.*

In modern conversation we often talk about the ego as the part of us that is selfish and focused only on our own pleasure or gain. We become concerned with what we have and how we are seen over what we can give and connecting with our community as a whole.

The personality is how we distinguish ourselves from others in terms of how we think, feel, and behave. We individuate ourselves by certain characteristics that make up our personality.

In this section you can learn more about how you see yourSelf, how you think others see you, and if what you believe matches well with your behavior.

I am afraid of . . .

My intuition tells me . . .

I am most observant when . . .

I'm critical when it comes to . . .

I protect myself by . . .

The person I blame the most is . . .

The person who gives me feedback about myself is . . .

I accept feedback from . . .

I am defensive around . . .

Socially, I tend to be . . .

When I am alone, I . . .

I learn from . . .

What others don't understand about me is . . .

Others are critical of me about . . .

My feelings are . . .

I think too much about . . .

When I am judgmental . . .

When I assert myself . . .

I am chaotic around . . .

I'll never change my . . .

I am afraid of . . .

My memory is . . .

I am defensive when . . .

I like to spend time with . . .

I like to spend time doing . . .

My thinking . . .

Health

The chakras are like little energy centers of vital information. The issues related to your health are included your chakras.

As we've seen before, Caroline Myss says that "your biography is your biology." This means that what happens in your emotional life ends up in your physical body.

I share more about this in the Fifth Chakra. I've included some emotional Soul stems that are significant to your health in this section.

To intuitively read your health, do the **Grounding Meditation** that you bookmarked. Before the Intuitive Reading Process, you will also want to do a Body Scan.

BODY SCAN INSTRUCTIONS

Close your eyes, take a deep breath, ground, and focus on your body beginning at the top of your head.

Just scan your body downward being aware of any tension, unusual sensation or any place that you feel stuck energy, discomfort or pain. Just notice this.

Then continue to the Intuitive Reading Process. Ask for a symbol related to your health.

Health issues that may arise from third chakra imbalances.

- Eating disorders such as anorexia, bulimia and malnutrition
- Digestive disorders, indigestion, and ulcers
- Pancreatitis, hypoglycemia, and diabetes
- Gall bladder issues, gallstones
- Liver problems including cirrhosis, hepatitis, and liver cancer
- Colon and intestinal problems, spleen problems
- Hiatal hernia
- Adrenal fatigue
- Muscle spasms and muscular disorders
- Chronic fatigue
- Hypertension

My body craves . . .

I overeat when . . .

My hunger is . . .

I am afraid to eat because . . .

My body tells me to . . .

The cells of my body . . .

When I feel fat, I . . .

When I feel skinny, I . . .

My body is starving for . . .

I feel victimized when . . .

I would feel better about myself if . . .

I'm easily manipulated by . . .

I'm passive when . . .

The person to blame is . . .

When I am unreliable . . .

I try to control . . .

I'm aggressive when . . .

When I dominate (name) then . . .

My need to be right affects . . .

Others see me as stubborn when . . .

I can't stomach . . .

My tiredness . . .

My pain . . .

If I were rested . . .

I don't trust . . .

I am intimidated by . . .

I intimidate others by . . .

My low self-esteem causes . . .

I criticize . . .

When (name) criticizes me . . .

I am enmeshed with . . .

When I was enmeshed with . . .

I manipulate . . .

I feel emotionally manipulated by . . .

Affirmations for the Third Chakra

- I stand in my power.
- I empower others.
- I express myself fully.
- I love mySelf.
- I can be separate and connected.
- I am happy, healthy and joyful.

There is more information on Chakra Three on my website, including information on how to balance your Third Chakra.

http://energymedicinedna.com/chakra-three

CHAKRA FOUR

We accept the love we think we deserve.
~ *Stephen Chbosky*

THE FOURTH CHAKRA is the Heart Chakra which relates to love, self-love, love of others, love of God/Goddess, affinity, loneliness and commitment, forgiveness and compassion, hope and trust. Health issues related to the heart chakra involve the circulatory system, immune system, thymus, heart, breast, lungs, ribs, and chest. The major issues of the fourth chakra are loving and being loved.

When you are looking at your chakra psychically, here are some images you may see that represent the fourth chakra:

- *Cracked heart* – represents pain or broken relationship

- *Heart tied with barbed wire* – represents an angry heart, over-protected heart, being stuck, tied up or feeling like you can't leave

- *Group of people dancing and singing* – represents loving humanity, being connected, feeling safe in groups

Self Love

So often your perception of yourSelf comes from how others have seen and treated you as a child. As a young child, you are not only vulnerable, you are impressionable and make decisions early on about your worth. We emulate those around us and attempt to get our needs met for love and belonging. This can set up a belief about yourSelf that will ultimately change with the experiences and attitudes you have throughout your life. The generation in which you were raised and your culture also affects your view of yourSelf and self-love.

What I believe about myself is . . .

What I value about myself is . . .

The biggest trauma I experienced was . . .

If I forgive [name] I am afraid . . .

I long to open my heart, but . . .

I still need to heal the memory of . . .

I use my past to sabotage myself by . . .

The person who controls me by their pain is . . .

They do this by . . .

I respond to this person by . . .

When I am in pain, I . . .

I protect myself by . . .

I can learn to protect myself by . . .

If I were emotionally healthy I would have to . . .

If I were emotionally healthy I would lose . . .

What I fear the most about being healthy is . . .

I long to open up my heart to . . .

I'm afraid if I open my heart, then . . .

What intimacy means to me is . . .

I was most intimate with . . .

I am most intimate with . . .

I want to be more intimate with . . .

What I need to do to open my heart is . . .

My heart aches when I think about . . .

I feel selfish when . . .

I feel guilty when . . .

If I focus on myself . . .

Affinity and Compassion for Others

Living in relationship can bring the greatest joy and also the most excruciating pain. So often you learn the most important lessons from those with whom you desire the deepest connection. Keeping an open heart can be challenging. Healing a hardened heart can take time.

As you delve into your heart with these Soul stems, be sure to have support. This can be from a loved one, a friend, or a group that you join that is also journaling with *Live Intuitively*. When you allow yourSelf to feel your full range of feelings, your heart stays healthy. When you stuff your feelings, your heart hardens and the energy gets stored in your body and can create illness.

My clients know that I am an advocate of feeling your feelings. Crying can be such an incredible healing experience. When you feel pain and don't allow yourSelf to cry, you often cover it with anger. If you are afraid to cry because you are sure you will never stop crying – truly – you will be able to stop. For those of you who cry more than you like, healing does happen. You may need to learn to distract yourSelf at times to stop crying and then allow yourSelf to cry again when there is a quiet or private time. Eventually you master allowing yourSelf to cry and heal and also to close the door to the tears and be present to the situation at hand. You will gain control.

Your experience and your personality will determine how much time you spend in connection with others and your desire to serve others. These Soul stems will help you understand yourSelf more deeply.

When I met [name], I immediately knew . . .

What I desire from a relationship is . . .

The person I am the most hurt by is . . .

My heart aches when I think about . . .

I was hurt when . . .

I protect myself by . . .

I can learn to protect myself by . . .

The biggest trauma I have had is . . .

If I forgive, I am afraid . . .

I need forgiveness from . . .

What intimacy means to me is . . .

I am most intimate with . . .

I want to be more intimate with . . .

The person I trust with my heart is . . .

I've given my heart to . . .

I'll never give my heart to . . .

My heart was broken by . . .

I am so lonely when . . .

I cannot commit because . . .

My heart aches when I think about . . .

When I am in pain I . . .

I use my pain to control . . .

My past sabotages me by . . .

The person who controls me by their pain is . . .

I am fully alive when . . .

I give freely to . . .

My heart is happiest when . . .

My child-heart desires . . .

My connection with God/Goddess is . . .

I have to stop . . .

I am happier when I don't . . .

I love myself when I . . .

What I can do to heal is . . .

If I could choose, I would. . .

Forgiveness, Loneliness, and Commitment

When students ask me how to choose which Soul stems to use, I usually suggest they look them over and pick the one that scares them the most. This of course will give them the most healing. When I wrote the words forgiveness, loneliness, and commitment, I imagined that many of the most transformative and freeing experiences you will get will come from this section.

Forgiveness is such a powerful concept to master and is difficult for many. Remember that you can forgive someone and let them go so they no longer take up residency in your mind (and cells) without agreeing with them. Forgiveness does not mean you need to embrace the person or let them into your life. Setting a boundary is a healthy choice.

Sometimes I hear that if you love yourSelf, you will never be lonely. I don't agree with that statement. You can be a healthy, happy person and at times still feel lonely. Different personalities have different needs as far as connection with others goes. Some have a strong need for physical connection and touch. Others are very social and need to have a lot of people around. Even those who are self-sufficient have occasional bouts of loneliness.

When you explore commitment, know that you have choices and can change your mind. When I sit with clients who are struggling - ready to leave a marriage or a job - I ask them when they first knew this (marriage or job) was not right for them. Often they say it was the first day they met or before they married. They received a clear intuitive hit, but didn't listen. If you make a commitment and it goes against what your intuition says to you, listen to YourSelf.

Exploring forgiveness, loneliness and commitment will give you deep insight to yourSelf.

I still need to heal the memory of when ...

My heart really hurts when I think about ...

The person I am the most hurt by is ...

I am so angry at ...

I need to forgive ...

I use my pain to control ...

The person who controls me by their pain is ...

They do this by ...

I respond to this person by ...

I can learn to protect myself by ...

When I am in pain I ...

I use my pain to control ...

My past sabotages me by ...

The person who controls me by their pain is ...

If I were emotionally healthy I would have to . . .

If I were emotionally healthy I would lose . . .

Forgiveness means . . .

I need to forgive . . .

If I forgive, I am afraid . . .

I need forgiveness from . . .

The person who is working to forgive me is . . .

What I need to forgive myself for is . . .

I am so afraid to love because . . .

I don't care because . . .

I give so much to . . .

I feel so unappreciated when . . .

I am going to stop helping . . .

I feel rejected by . . .

I am suffocated by . . .

I can't communicate with . . .

You can't demand so much of me because . . .

I have nothing to give because . . .

You are not present to me when . . .

I am so jealous of . . .

I really envy . . .

I'm afraid if I open my heart, then . . .

What intimacy means to me is . . .

I was most intimate with . . .

I am most intimate with . . .

I want to be more intimate with . . .

My heart aches when I think about . . .

What I need to do to open my heart is . . .

I feel lonely when . . .

I'll never be happy again after . . .

The greatest commitment I've made is . . .

What I commit to myself is . . .

When [name] broke the commitment . . .

What commitment means is . . .

Today I will commit to . . .

Hope and Trust

Some of us are eternally hopeful and live our lives as if our dreams will be fulfilled. Others are more skeptical and cautious.

You may sometimes feel that hope and trust just happen to you and you are responding to a natural sense of being. What I would venture is that it is your **thinking** that creates what you *feel* and being hopeful and trusting are well within your control. I know that having been hurt by someone can make you distrustful, at least of that person.

When you activate your intuition, you have a good connection with yourSelf, you are more able to get a sense of who to trust and who not to trust. When you are congruent with yourSelf, when you are true to your beliefs and you do what you say you will do, you learn to trust yourSelf.

This is a great exercise to explore the boundaries of your beliefs.

If I were hopeful ...

My fear of being hopeful is ...

What hope means to me is ...

I long to open up my heart to ...

What I need to do to open my heart is ...

My heart aches when I think about ...

I long to open my heart, but if I do ...

I don't trust ...

When I don't trust myself, I ...

The reason I can't trust [name] is ...

I'll never trust ...

'Trust isn't earned' means ...

My heart aches when I think about ...

I was betrayed by ...

When [name] betrayed me, I ...

I would trust [name] if ...

When I trusted [name] ...

I feel vengeful when I think about ...

If I could do it over again, I would ...

In order for me to trust, I have to ...

In order to forgive, you have to ...

In order for me to forgive, I have to ...

Spiritual Love

What it means to be spiritual is sometimes perplexing. I have seen people who are known to be spiritual behave in ways that surprise me. I am sure others think that way about me as well. We are all human. You are in a process of enlightenment, wherever you are on the path. Sometimes when I talk about spirituality, I say it is like air. It is everywhere and I don't even think about it. It just is.

When you think of spiritual love, this can be of a soul mate or your relationship with God/Goddess, or with others. It is such a personal decision how you experience and define Spiritual Love.

The beliefs you had as a child may have developed and become stronger, or may have changed as you were influenced by others in your life. Your expanded awareness shifted your beliefs and that can be enlightening!

When I was a child I believed . . .

Church has been for me . . .

I quit going to church because . . .

My description of God/Goddess is . . .

God/Goddess shows up in my life as . . .

I felt so hurt by God/Goddess when . . .

When I am in pain, I turn to . . .

I protect myself by . . .

I felt betrayed by God/Goddess when . . .

If God/Goddess loved me then . . .

What I was taught as a child is . . .

I feel comforted by God/Goddess when . . .

Meditation for me is . . .

How I meditate is . . .

The reason I meditate is . . .

My religion teaches . . .

I am comforted by my religion because . . .

I was hurt by my religion because . . .

What my parents didn't understand about me . . .

I trust God/Goddess when . . .

I don't trust God/Goddess because . . .

I am connected to God/Goddess when . . .

I feel disconnected from God/Goddess when . . .

The meaning of sin is . . .

Others judge me by . . .

Others judge me because . . .

I judge others when . . .

If you were spiritual, you would . . .

Prayer for me is . . .

How I pray is . . .

The reason I pray is . . .

My most incredible spiritual experience was when . . .

My spiritual friend [name] gifts me by . . .

I serve others by . . .

I isolate because . . .

Others serve me by . . .

God/Goddess guides me by . . .

I trust guidance without "proof" because . . .

I don't trust guidance without "proof" because . . .

I follow guidance without attachment to the outcome because. . .

I follow guidance but want to know the outcome because. . . My greatest fear of following Divine guidance is . . .

My prayers consist of asking for . . .

I am afraid to ask to be guided by Divine guidance without specifics when . . .

Health

The chakras are like little energy centers of vital information. The issues related to your health are included your chakras.

Thinking back to Caroline Myss's "your biography is your biology", this means that what happens in your emotional life, ends up in your physical body. I share more about this in the Fifth Chakra chapter. I've included some emotional Soul stems that are significant to your health in this section.

To intuitively read your health, do the **Grounding Meditation** that you bookmarked. Before the Intuitive Reading Process, you will also want to do a Body Scan.

BODY SCAN INSTRUCTIONS

Close your eyes, take a deep breath, ground, and focus on your body - beginning at the top of your head.

Just scan your body downward, being aware of any tension, unusual sensation, or any place that you feel stuck energy, discomfort, or pain. Just notice this.

Then continue to the Intuitive Reading Process. Ask for a symbol related to your health.

Health issues that may arise from fourth chakra imbalances.

- Congestive heart failure, heart attack, chest pain
- Lung cancer
- Bronchial pneumonia
- Arteriosclerosis, peripheral vascular insufficiency
- Sunken chest
- Shortness of breath
- Asthma and allergies
- Breast cancer and disorders
- Issues of the shoulders, upper back, and chest
- Immune system deficiency
- Problems with circulation

If I were the best I could be I would . . .

My heart pounds when . . .

I feel tingling in my heart when . . .

I am afraid my physical heart will . . .

My physical heart wants to tell me . . .

Depression makes me . . .

I am anxious when . . .

I cannot breathe when . . .

My lungs hurt when . . .

My lungs want to tell me . . .

I am emotionally allergic to . . .

My physical allergy is to . . .

If I were to describe my breasts, they would be . . .

My breasts want to tell me . . .

My chest sinks when I think of . . .

My chest wants to tell me . . .

Who I nurture and feed the most is . . .

My shoulders often feel . . .

The person who I need to knock off my shoulder is . . .

My shoulders want to tell me . . .

My immune system will increase when I . . .

My immune system wants to tell me . . .

My circulation slows down when I . . .

I can increase my circulation by . . .

My circulation wants to tell me . . .

I am critical of . . .

I judge . . .

If I stop being critical and judgmental . . .

I long to open my heart but if I do . . .

I hardened my heart when . . .

My heart is resistant to . . .

The greatest loss was . . .

I withdraw from . . .

I isolate when . . .

I am critical of . . .

I feel judged by . . .

My heart is closed when I judge . . .

Affirmations for the Fourth Chakra

- I am worthy of and receive love.
- I love myself wholeheartedly.
- I share with and love others.
- Love is abundant and available to me.
- My heart vibrates with love openly.
- I am happy, healthy, and joyful.

There is more information on Chakra Four on my website, including information on how to balance your Fourth Chakra.

http://energymedicinedna.com/ chakra-four

CHAKRA FIVE

Doctor, I'd like a bottle of placebo please.
~ *Candess M. Campbell*

THE FIFTH CHAKRA is the Throat chakra, which relates to communication, choice, strength of will, capacity to make decisions, speech, manifesting, individual needs, and self – expression. Health issues related to the throat chakra involve the thyroid gland, endocrine system, respiratory system, throat, neck, ears, jaw, mouth, teeth, gums, and tongue. The major issues of the fifth chakra are choice and speaking and hearing the truth.

When you are looking at your chakra psychically, here are some images you may see that represent the fifth chakra:

- *Cotton in the mouth* – represents someone keeping you from talking, clouded communication, inability or unwillingness to be clear

- *Clenching teeth* – anger at someone or something, communicating with anger, passive aggressiveness

- *Vomiting* – spewing out anger, histrionic behavior, purging the past

If you are curious, I share one of my own journal writings where I focused on the fifth chakra. You can find it in the Guideline for Hosting Journal Groups under the Intuition section.

Most situations that arise in your life will be related to the information in the fifth chakra. Communication is integral to living happy and healthy lives.

Communication, Speech, and Self-Expression

The throat chakra deals with communication with yourSelf, with others and the God/Goddess of your heart. Giving voice to your beliefs and sharing from your heart can improve your self-esteem.

Communication with others can be difficult, especially if you want something from them or they want you to behave differently. Years of counseling has taught me that, if you want to be heard, often it is helpful to hear the other person's agenda first.

Once they feel heard, they are more likely to listen. Of course, this doesn't mean there will be agreement. When I do psychic readings with clients, the chakras that need the most attention are usually the third (power) and fifth (communication and choice.) Most often, these two chakras are related.

When you are intuitively reading yourSelf and you get a symbol in this chakra, you may want to check for a symbol in your third chakra too.

When you know yourSelf well and you meditate on a regular basis to clear your energy, expressing yourSelf can be fun and playful. When it's difficult to express yourSelf, you may find that other people are throwing energy at you and trying to keep you from speaking. When I intuitively read clients, I often see this in the fifth chakra. An image that comes up often is the image of cotton. I see an image of cotton being stuffed in the mouth or down the throat. At times I see the cotton being put in the fifth chakra from the back of the neck. This means that the person is throwing energy at you indirectly from behind you. They are either trying to keep you from talking or from getting your own information. Using the 12 Minute Chakra Clearing CD[1] will clear other people's energy from your energy field and protect you from this interference.

My greatest judgment is about ...

Other than myself, the person I judge the most is ...

I judge myself unmercifully about ...

Other than myself, I expect too much from ...

What I expect from this person is ...

I expect myself to ...

This expectation causes me to ...

If I were to let go of expectation, then ...

If I were to let go of judgment ...

I continually ruminate about ...

Because this happened, I feel ...

Because this happened, I believe ...

The decision I made about myself is ...

I can't let go of this worry because if I do ...

I don't trust that things happen for a purpose when ...

I don't trust myself because ...

I trust God/Goddess when ...

I don't trust God/Goddess because ...

I am shy around ...

I don't have a voice because ...

If I shared how I felt, then ...

Speaking in public would ...

When others tell me to speak up, I ...

I can express myself openly and honestly with ...

I don't express myself openly and honestly with ...

I have a problem expressing myself openly and honestly when ...

My words get messed up when I talk to ...

I keep secrets from ...

The scariest secret I won't share is ...

Secrecy creates problems for me with ...

I can't stop talking because ...

When others tell me I talk too much or too loud, I ...

Paying attention and listening is hard because ...

When I filter my words, I ...

I have to talk about others' lives because ...

Gossiping gives me ...

I finish other people's sentences because ...

When others speak slowly, I ...

What I can't share with others is ...

I am so confused about ...

I tend to waiver when ...

What I expect from this person is ...

I expect myself to ...

This expectation causes me to ...

If I were to let go of expectation, then ...

If I were to let go of judgment ...

I continually ruminate about why things happened. I do this most about ...

I can't let go of worry because if I do ...

A strong-willed person is ...

Willpower means ...

The person who controls me the most is ...

I let this happen because ...

The person I attempt to control is . . .

I do this because . . .

I can express myself openly and honestly with . . .

Choice, Will and Decision Making

The fifth chakra governs the choices you make, including the choices you make about your health. It is in this chakra that there is the struggle between your self-will and turning your will over to God/Goddess.

A strong-willed person is . . .

Willpower means . . .

I don't trust that things happen for a purpose when . . .

The person who controls my will the most is . . .

I let this happen because . . .

The person I attempt to control is . . .

I do this because . . .

I can express myself openly and honestly with . . .

I don't express myself openly and honestly with . . .

I don't express myself openly and honestly when . . .

God/Goddess guides me by . . .

I trust guidance without "proof" because . . .

I don't trust guidance without "proof" because . . .

I follow guidance without attachment to the outcome because. . .

I follow guidance but want to know the outcome because. . .

My greatest fear of following Divine guidance is . . .

My prayers consist of asking for . . .

I am afraid to ask to be guided by Divine guidance without specifics when . . .

I lose control of my willpower when . . .

In my life, I know I need to change . . .

I don't take action because . . .

My health would improve if . . .

I am afraid to do this because. . .

If I took this action, then. . .

I lose control of my willpower when . . .

What I need to change . . .

I don't take action because . . .

The decision I need to make now is . . .

I could decide, if only . . .

I am dishonest about . . .

If I told the truth, then . . .

Dishonesty gives me power because . . .

My greatest judgment is about . . .

Other than myself, the person I judge the most is . . .

I judge myself unmercifully about . . .

Other than myself, I expect too much from . . .

The negative decision I made about myself is . . .

The positive decision I made about myself is . . .

Health

The chakras are like little energy centers of vital information. The issues related to your health are included your chakra. Caroline Myss says "your biography is your biology." This means that what happens in your emotional life ends up in your physical body. I've included some emotional Soul stems that are significant to your health in this section.

I have a situation from my own life where a significant relationship ended abruptly. I was not able to communicate with the person to understand what happened and to have closure. It was extremely painful. I covered the pain with anger, which is common for us all. The anger was stuck in my throat (couldn't communicate with the person) and it ran through my body for several months. It took a toll on my fifth chakra.

As a result, eight years later I found there was a growth on my thyroid the size of a plum. This is an example of how emotional energy that gets stuck can turn into physical illness.

To intuitively read your health, do the **Grounding Meditation** that you bookmarked. Before the Intuitive Reading Process, you will also want to do a Body Scan.

BODY SCAN INSTRUCTIONS

Close your eyes, take a deep breath, ground, and focus on your body - beginning at the top of your head.

Just scan your body downward, being aware of any tension, unusual sensation, or any place that you feel stuck energy, discomfort, or pain. Just notice this.

Then continue to the Intuitive Reading Process. Ask for a symbol related to your health.

Health issues that may arise from fifth chakra imbalances.

- TMJ (Temporomandibular Joint Disorders)
- Hypothyroidism, hyperthyroidism, thyroiditis, thyroid cancer, Hashimoto's, Grave's disease
- Chronic sore throat
- Mouth ulcers
- Gum difficulties
- Sinus problems
- Throat cancer
- Laryngitis
- Joint problems
- Neck problems
- Swollen glands

My throat feels sore when . . .

I get a sour taste in my mouth when . . .

I "burn to bitch" [at/when/about] What my throat has to tell me is . . .

My gums burn when . . .

I don't floss my gums because . . .

My gums want to tell me . . .

My joints ache when . . .

The joint that hurts the most is . . .

If I listened to my joints, I would know . . .

My thyroid supports me by . . .

I am angry at my thyroid because . . .

If I listened to my thyroid, I would understand . . .

If I could love myself more, I would . . .

I am fully alive when . . .

My heart is happiest when . . .

My child-heart desires . . .

The greatest loss was . . .

I feel judged by . . .

My heart is closed when I judge . . .

I feel rejected by . . .

I can't communicate with . . .

My heart pounds when . . .

I feel tingling in my heart when . . .

Affirmations for the Fifth Chakra

- I listen and hear the truth.
- I express my truth clearly.
- I make decisions intuitively.
- I make healthy decisions regarding my health.
- I align my will with God/Goddess.
- I am happy, healthy, and joyful.

There is more information on Chakra Five on my website, including information on how to balance your Fifth Chakra.

http://energymedicinedna.com/chakra-five

CHAKRA SIX

Intuition will tell the thinking mind where to look next.

~ Jonas Salk

THE SIXTH CHAKRA is the Brow chakra, associated with the third eye which relates to insight, clear seeing, clairvoyance, intuition, perception, imagination, self-evaluation, intellect, and wisdom. Health issues related to the Brow chakra involve the eyes, brain, pituitary and pineal glands, lymphatic and endocrine systems, and sinuses. The major issues of the sixth chakra are the ability and right to see clearly.

When you are looking at your chakra psychically, here are some images you may see that represent the sixth chakra:

- *Spinning image above the head* – represents being stuck in thinking and trying to figure things out, overly trying to connect with guides or get spiritual information

- *Guide or Ascended master* – represents the guide that is there for you

- *Image of what you are creating in your life*

Clairvoyance and Intuition

There are four ways to develop your clairvoyance.

- Clairaudience is clear-hearing

- Claircognizance is clear-knowing

- Clairsentience is clear-feeling

- Clairvoyance is clear-seeing

I have been teaching this information for over 20 years and there is more information in videos on my website.

http://energymedicinedna.com

Clairaudience is when you have a voice that gives you information. An example is the one I gave earlier in the book about waking up and being told to go to the Grand Canyon.

Claircognizance is clear knowing. You may have experienced this when you first met someone and you automatically knew something about them that they didn't share. What happens to me a lot is, when I am watching a detective drama I immediately know who did it. I've learned not to blurt it out in front of others!

When I was a child, I watched a TV show called Hollywood Squares. Of the nine squares where celebrities sat, there was one "secret square." I was always able to guess who was sitting in the secret square. It wasn't until many years later I learned that not everyone could do this.

Many of us experience Clairsentience, which is clear feeling, before developing the other intuitive abilities. One day my friend and previous assistant, Marc, was in town. He had moved to New Delhi, India and started a business and was back in Spokane visiting his family. We planned to meet at Starbucks and he chose one on the north side of town. I was on my way, driving through downtown and I got a "hit" or a weird sensation in my gut. I pulled over and saw that he had recently sent me a text saying he decided to go downtown and could I meet him at Starbucks on Riverside. It was perfect. I was one minute away. Had I not gotten the hit, I would have ended up wasting about 40 minutes in travel time. I am so grateful for clairsentience!

Clairvoyance is clear seeing. This is where the visual comes in that I taught you. Another example of clairvoyance would be if someone asks you where they left their keys and you get an image of it in your mind. One time I was sitting at the kitchen bar writing and I wanted to quote the "Love is patient, Love is kind" passage from the Bible. As I searched through the Bible, I couldn't find the passage, so I closed my eyes and immediately got the vision of 1 Corinthians 13:4-8.

This is where having your journal with you at all times comes in. When you get these intuitive "hits," be sure to write them down. It is this continued awareness of how many times your intuition supports you that you develop it even more!

My intuition tells me . . .

When I listen, I hear that I should . . .

My guide tells me that . . .

[Name] who passed over tells me . . .

What I need to say to [name of deceased] is . . .

I sense [name of deceased] by . . .

When I trusted my intuition . . .

My psychic told me . . .

My future holds . . .

I cannot imagine . . .

If I were to remember my dreams . . .

My dreams tell me to . . .

I fantasize that . . .

My last nightmare . . .

My self-talk says for me to . . .

What I know to be true is . . .

When I listen to my gut . . .

The image that guides me was . . .

When I don't listen to my intuition . . .

Self-evaluation

Since the advent of the self-help movement people have the tools to self-evaluate. People are encouraged to look inward and adjust their behaviors. Prior to this self-reflection was limited to philosophy and ethics, which were mostly academic.

There are so many great tools to for self-study. There is the Myers-Briggs, the Enneagram and many other personality tests. Being a student of psychology, as much as I love these tests, I believe journaling will give you a deeper inner view of yourself. Journey on . . . I mean journal on!

I tend to be insensitive when . . .

The reason I am stuck in the past is . . .

What I cannot remember is . . .

I know I am in denial about . . .

A value I won't let go of is . . .

When I am rigid, I feel . . .

My hidden obsession is . . .

I continually worry about . . .

I make up stories in my head about . . .

I am compulsive about . . .

I lose my concentration when . . .

When others say I don't remember . . .

My greatest fear is . . .

I avoid looking at my behavior because . . .

Self-evaluation means that I need to . . .

I am resistive when/to . . .

I try not to think too much because . . .

Smart people are . . .

I am insecure when . . .

I am unworthy because . . .

I don't deserve . . .

I don't believe . . .

You can't convince me that . . .

It's not my fault when . . .

My thinking and feelings don't match about . . .

I am incongruent about . . .

Wisdom and Intellect

There was a time when I thought wisdom only came with age. Today I believe character is also important. You have many past lives and my experience as a psychic reader has given me insight to many students and clients. I have clearly been able to see that some of the wisest people I know have had several lifetimes learning how to master being a Spirit in a body.

I am sure you have heard of someone being an "old soul." Maybe people have said that about you. Whether it has come from your age, great teachers, or lifetimes you have lived, it is time to tap into your wisdom and intellect. You may be amazed at what you find.

What I know I should be doing is . . .

What I know I should not be doing is . . .

I am truly right about . . .

I won't compromise on . . .

The best way to handle people is . . .

Resistance makes me . . .

The greatest teacher was/is . . .

What I have learned that I value is . . .

What I can share with others is . . .

What is most meaningful is . . .

Intelligence is useful when . . .

I use my intellect to . . .

What wisdom I can share is . . .

What I heard that is the most wise is . . .

If I were wiser, I would . . .

What I want to share with my children is . . .

What I have learned from my life is . . .

If I were to write a book, it would be . . .

Health

The chakras are like little energy centers of vital information. The issues related to your health are included your chakras. Caroline Myss says "your biography is your biology." This means that what happens in your emotional life, ends up in your physical body. I share about this in the Fifth Chakra. I've included some emotional Soul stems that are significant to your health in this section.

To intuitively read your health, do the **Grounding Meditation** that you bookmarked. Before the Intuitive Reading Process, you will also want to do a Body Scan.

BODY SCAN INSTRUCTIONS

Close your eyes, take a deep breath, ground, and focus on your body - beginning at the top of your head.

Just scan your body downward, being aware of any tension, unusual sensation, or any place that you feel stuck energy, discomfort, or pain. Just notice this.

Then continue to the Intuitive Reading Process. Ask for a symbol related to your health.

Health issues that may arise from Sixth chakra imbalances.

- Headaches
- Upper and frontal sinus issues
- Brain tumors, hemorrhage
- Stroke
- Neurological disturbances
- Poor eyesight, glaucoma, cataracts
- Blindness and deafness
- Full spinal difficulties
- Learning disabilities
- Seizures

I get headaches because . . .

My head hurts when . . .

I don't listen well to . . .

I don't listen well because I . . .

What I don't want to hear is . . .

I can't see well when . . .

I can't see well because . . .

What I don't want to see is . . .

Because of my brain injury . . .

If my brain worked better I would . . .

Since my stroke . . .

My stroke allows me to . . .

My ADD/ADHD causes . . .

Because of ADD/ADHD, I get away with . . .

My dementia . . .

Not remembering allows me to . . .

My chronic pain . . .

If I were not in pain I would . . .

After my coma . . .

Because of dyslexia . . .

My seizures . . .

I can increase my immune system by . . .

The inflammation causes . . .

Without migraines I would . . .

I get migraines when . . .

I can't sleep when . . .

If I could only sleep, then . . .

When I can't sleep I . . .

After my seizures . . .

I make excuses about . . .

I love myself even though . . .

Affirmations for the Sixth Chakra

- I use my clear intuition daily.

- I am open to my wisdom from within.

- I balance my intellect with compassion.

- I evaluate myself with pure love.

- I am sensitive to my needs and those of others.

- I am happy, healthy and joyful.

There is more information on Chakra Six on my website, including information on how to balance your Sixth Chakra.

http://energymedicinedna.com/chakra-six

CHAKRA SEVEN

Children show me in their playful smiles
the Divine in everyone.

~ Michael Jackson

THE SEVENTH CHAKRA is the Crown Chakra which relates to the Divine, Higher Self, enlightenment, consciousness, knowingness, values, ethics, courage, selflessness, meditation, faith and inspiration, spirituality, and devotion. Health issues related to the crown chakra involve the muscular system, skeletal system, and skin. These could be coma or amnesia, migraines, anxiety, depression, strokes, epilepsy and brain tumors, Parkinson's, ALS (Lou Gehrig's disease), MS (Multiple Sclerosis), dementia, or Alzheimer's. The major issues of the seventh chakra are the right to learn and to know.

When you are looking at your chakra psychically, here are some images you may see that represent the seventh chakra:

- *Guide or Ascended master* – represents the guide that is there for you
- *A loved one who has crossed over*
- *Situation related to ethics or values*

Knowingness, Values, and Ethics

Over time, you become shaped by your environment and, in addition to your natural personality and temperament, hopefully you live your life with a sense of what you believe and what is true for you.

What I know to be true is . . .

What I thought was important when I was 10 was . . .

What I believed as a child that is different today is . . .

What I want to teach my children is . . .

What I value most is . . .

I would never . . .

I compromised myself when I . . .

I was so embarrassed when . . .

The memory that haunts me from childhood is . . .

Three words that describe my code of honor are . . .

The part of me I have compromised the most is my . . .

What I value most from my childhood is . . .

What my child self wants to do more of is . . .

The most powerful choice I have made is . . .

If I were truthful . . .

When I lie I feel . . .

When I am truthful I feel . . .

When I have money, I can . . .

What integrity means is . . .

My incongruence affects my integrity by . . .

People who say one thing and do another . . .

I don't keep my word when . . .

When I don't keep my word, I . . .

Compassion keeps me from . . .

Compassion supports my character by . . .

I am most compassionate when . . .

I don't feel any compassion for . . .

Ethically, I cross the line when . . .

What ethics mean to me is . . .

Ethics don't concern me because . . .

Other people's ethics bother me when . . .

I am most loyal to . . .

[Name]'s loyalty to me is . . .

If I were loyal, I would not have . . .

If I were loyal, I would . . .

I ended a friendship because . . .

My respect for myself is . . .

I don't respect . . .

I don't respect people who . . .

To earn my respect you have to . . .

I lost respect for [name] when . . .

[Name] does not respect me by . . .

I would give respect if . . .

I share easily with [name] because . . .

I am don't share with [name] because . . .

I feel guilty for not sharing my . . .

[Name] expects me to share . . .

The truth is . . .

I don't believe when you say . . .

I don't tell the truth because . . .

It's important to tell the truth when . . .

Courage

For some reason the word courage had so many inaccurate connotations for me, I decided to Google it! What I found was that courage means "the ability to do something that frightens one" and "strength in the face of pain or grief."

When I thought of courage, other than the cowardly lion image, I believe that today it has a lot to do with the ability to say something difficult to someone - difficult because they don't want to hear it. Too often I sit with clients who have not shared honestly with a spouse or a parent for many years and, after suffering in silence, they find themselves regretting the decision.

My desire is to help others live intuitively, to follow their gut and speak clearly and honestly. So often, when you slow down and begin to hear yourSelf, you can make choices that save a lifetime of pain.

What I wished I had shared is . . .

What I said that empowered me was when . . .

When I stood up to [name], I . . .

What I just couldn't do is . . .

I pushed through and completed . . .

Even though it hurt, I . . .

When I was grieving, I couldn't . . .

Painful as it was, I forgave [name] when . . .

I feel good about rescuing [name] from . . .

I don't really care at all about . . .

The message I would share about courage is . . .

Had I been more courageous, I would have . . .

Someday, I have to . . .

I forgive myself for not being able to . . .

I am so grateful to [name] for . . .

Inspiration, Faith, Spirituality and Devotion

I am so inspired by [name] because . . .

If I were more like [name] I would . . .

I believe faithfully that . . .

When I talk to [name], I feel like I can . . .

To become inspired, I . . .

In I were more inspired I would . . .

The person I have total faith in is . . .

Even without information, I totally trust that . . .

My belief in God/Goddess leaves me thinking . . .

I trust implicitly that . . .

Spirituality means . . .

Spiritual people are able to . . .

What I believe about God/Goddess is . . .

If I could talk to God/Goddess I would ask . . .

I would be more kind if I . . .

I don't deserve because I . . .

If God/Goddess loved me I would . . .

If I could connect with God/Goddess, I would . . .

I should be punished because . . .

Hell is . . .

I believe angels . . .

When I die . . .

Heaven is . . .

I feel alone when . . .

My prayers are . . .

I can contact God/Goddess by . . .

God/Goddess only listens . . .

Church feels like . . .

When others don't believe . . .

God/Goddess guides me by . . .

I trust guidance without "proof" because . . .

I don't trust guidance without "proof" because . . .

I follow guidance without attachment to the outcome because. . .

I follow guidance but want to know the outcome because. . .

My greatest fear of following Divine guidance is . . .

My prayers consist of asking for . . .

I am afraid to ask to be guided by Divine guidance without specifics when . . .

Health

The chakras are like little energy centers of vital information. The issues related to your health are included your chakras. Caroline Myss says "your biography is your biology." This means that what happens in your emotional life ends up in your physical body. I share more about this in the Fifth Chakra. I've included some emotional Soul stems that are significant to your health in this section.

To intuitively read your health, do the **Grounding Meditation** that you bookmarked. Before the Intuitive Reading Process, you will also want to do a Body Scan.

BODY SCAN INSTRUCTIONS

Close your eyes, take a deep breath, ground, and focus on your body - beginning at the top of your head.

Just scan your body downward, being aware of any tension, unusual sensation, or any place that you feel stuck energy, discomfort, or pain. Just notice this.

Then continue to the Intuitive Reading Process. Ask for a symbol related to your health.

Health issues that may arise from seventh chakra imbalances:

- Endocrine related disorders
- Central nervous system disorders
- Learning Disabilities
- Dissociation
- Spiritual addiction or cynicism
- Depression
- Anxiety

I lose control of my willpower when . . .

In my life, I know I need to change . . .

I don't take action because . . .

My health would improve if . . .

I am afraid to do this because. . .

If I took this action, then. . .

I am extremely sensitive to . . .

I am overwhelmed by . . .

When I am over-stimulated, others . . .

Nothing seems to matter anymore since . . .

Depression affects me by making me . . .

I become so anxious when . . .

I deal with my depression by . . .

I deal with my anxiety by . . .

If depression is anger buried, I would be angry at . . .

If anxiety is being in the future, I worry about . . .

I continually resist . . .

I am exhausted from . . .

If I were not so resistant, I would . .

If I had more energy, I would . . .

I use my illness to control . . .

[Name] is so angry at me because . . .

I would be willing to forgive if . . .

Affirmations for the Seventh Chakra

- I am one with the Divine Light.
- I am guided by integrity.
- I am guided by my inner Wisdom.
- I am always learning and integrating.
- I balance my spirituality with being grounded.
- I am happy, healthy, and joyful.

There is more information on Chakra Seven on my website, including information on how to balance your Seventh Chakra.

http://energymedicinedna.com/chakra- seven-power-of-consciousness

CHAKRA EIGHT

How people treat you is their karma;
how you react is yours.
~ *Wayne W. Dyer*

THE EIGHTH CHAKRA is the first of the Spiritual Chakras and is a combination of the other chakras. It sits above the seventh chakra about two feet. The chakra is the gateway to yourSelf beyond your physical self. It contains karmic residue and, when you open it, it brings up patterns to clear that no longer serve you. It also opens up your spiritual awareness to your Higher Self, your Guides, and your Oneness with all that is.

Opening the eighth chakra is an ascension process. The energy can be intense and, as your psychic abilities increase, you may feel ungrounded. You will experience easier access to ideas, concepts, and abilities that you have not had before. You will be more connected to your Higher Self and guides will begin to show up for you. You will begin to have more "downloads."

Two ways to experience a download are these.

1. Having an experience of information coming to you and then feeling like you are in a daze. You may not be aware of what the information is at all.

2. Becoming aware of information immediately with a sense that it just dropped down from the heavens into your mind.

During this process you may find that a lot is coming up to emotionally and physically clear. How much disruption you experience will depend on how much of the past you have to clear. You may experience difficulty in relationships, jobs, and your health. To help you get through this opening process it is important that you practice being grounded. You can use the 12 Minute Energy Healing Meditation[2] I offer on my website. Getting massages, taking a footbath with Epsom Salts (only 20 minutes), and taking electrolytes can help.

The eighth chakra gives you an awareness that you belong to a larger community than just the human community. It is a transition to Oneness! As you open the eighth chakra it supports the healing of the Earth planet. At this point you may want to look into activating your DNA. You have two strands of DNA in your physical body, but there are many more strands in your etheric. With the Ascended Masters I have been activating DNA since 1991. Activation will help accelerate your intuition and much more. I liken it to a spiritual immune booster. You can find more information at.

http://energymedicinedna.com

When it is time for you to open the eighth chakra and you resist and it remains closed you may feel disconnected from the world. You may have a difficult time finding community and you feel isolated. You may feel you don't belong here.

When you are looking at your chakra psychically, here are some images you may see that represent the eighth chakra:

- *Betrayal or doing harm to someone –*
  represents karmic situation that needs cleared.

- *Guide or Ascended master* – represents the guide that is there for you.

- *Universe* – represents a connection with Oneness.

Eighth Chakra Sentence Stems

My dreams are telling me . . .

The person I need to clear with is . . .

The situation that still bothers me is . . .

I'm still stuck because . . .

What I resist is . . .

I need to make amends to . . .

My guide tells me . . .

If I pretended I had a guide, she would tell me . . .

The guides that support me say . . .

The spiritual gifts I have are . . .

Spiritually I'd like to develop . . .

My description of God/Goddess is . . .

God/Goddess shows up in my life is . . .

I felt so hurt by God/Goddess when . . .

When I am in pain, I turn to . . .

I protect myself by . . .

I felt betrayed by God/Goddess when . . .

If God/Goddess loved me then . . .

I feel comforted by God/Goddess when . . .

Meditation for me is . . .

How I meditate is . . .

The reason I meditate is . . .

I feel crazy when . . .

My community is . . .

I am isolated because . . .

My life purpose is . . .

If I were living my truth . . .

My new adventure is to . . .

Health

The chakras are like little energy centers of vital information. The issues related to your health are included your chakra. Caroline Myss says "your biography is your biology." This means that what happens in your emotional life, ends up in your physical body. I share more about this in the Fifth Chakra. I've included some emotional Soul stems that are significant to your health in this section.

To intuitively read your health, do the **Grounding Meditation** that you bookmarked. Before the Intuitive Reading Process, you will also want to do a Body Scan.

BODY SCAN INSTRUCTIONS

Close your eyes, take a deep breath, ground, and focus on your body - beginning at the top of your head.

Just scan your body downward, being aware of any tension, unusual sensation, or any place that you feel stuck energy, discomfort, or pain. Just notice this.

Then continue to the Intuitive Reading Process. Ask for a symbol related to your health.

Health issues that may arise from seventh chakra imbalances:

- Dissociation and confusion.
- Delusions.
- Cold feet or loss of feeling in feet.

- Feeling emotionally isolated.
- Lower back issues.

What confuses me the most is . . .

The dream that seemed so real was . . .

What scares me the most is . . .

I feel like I'm floating when . . .

What grounds me the most is . . .

I feel safe when . . .

I feel sane when . . .

I feel nurtured by . . .

The people who understand and support me are . . .

Affirmations for the Eighth Chakra

- I am receptive to my Higher Self.
- I am Divine Light.
- I am Love.
- I am One with the Universe.
- I am balanced and clear.
- I am happy, healthy and joyful.

Exploring Your Life Purpose

In 2008 when reading my clients in Japan, I began to understand more about one's life purpose. My Japanese clients often asked me to read their life purpose, but then they asked about their career. What became clear is many people see their life purpose mostly connected to the work they do in the world. The reality is, your life purpose encompasses your whole life. When I did the readings I began to see that the life purpose was directly related to one of the chakras.

~

Having explored your own chakras in this intuitive reading and journaling process, by now you should have an understanding of your own life purpose. Your life purpose is beyond what you want to do for work, but is more about how you relate to yourSelf, your friends and family and how you contribute in the world. Living your life purpose is about balancing yourSelf in your excess and deficiency.

An example is if your life purpose is aligned with your heart then you would balance yourSelf in the area of your heart chakra. Look over the signs of excess and deficiency and see where you are out of balance.

Signs of Deficiency in the fourth Chakra

- Being cold and withdrawn.
- Being critical and judgmental.
- Feeling isolated and lonely.
- Depression.
- Fear of intimacy, relationship problems.
- Lacking empathy.
- Narcissism.

Signs of Excess in the fourth Chakra

- Codependency (focusing on others rather than self).

- Having poor boundaries.

- Being demanding of others.

- Clinging to others.

- Being jealous of others.

- Behaving as a martyr.

After looking at these tendencies, think about your own life. Do you over-function in your family or at work? Do you do more than your share and then resent others for not doing more? Maybe you are critical and judgmental and tend to isolate rather than spending time with those who don't live up to your expectations.

The goal of understanding your life purpose is to bring yourSelf into balance. In the heart chakra this would mean having an open, loving heart while also practicing nurturing self-care.

You can find more information about the chakras at

http://energymedicinedna.com

Creating Your Future

When I teach manifesting the first and most important step is grounding. When you image on the mental reflective plane, it is important to be grounded so you can bring the images of what you desire into the physical form. By now you have practiced the **Grounding Meditation** and will be able to do this.

The second step is to begin to listen to what you say to

yourSelf. When you create your future you get clear on what you want to create, but the step many people miss is noticing all the thoughts that come up that challenge you. When this happens, use your journal and your journaling process to challenge these thoughts back!

Example:

> Imagine creating a relationship with a partner that is loving, kind, and supportive.

Self-talk

"I can't really attract someone."

> *Challenge: "I can attract someone who will love me. I am lovable and my qualities are..."*

"I'm too old/fat/sick."

> *Challenge: "I am loveable and I love myself fully. I will receive love by being open to..."*

"I don't really have time."

> *Challenge: "I am happier when I make time for love. I will do this by..."*

"Men/women leave me."

> *Challenge: "I am secure within myself and will attract...."*

"It's too painful."

> *Challenge: "I am open to being loved and receiving ...*

Your beliefs create your reality and your thoughts create your beliefs. Allow yourSelf in your journal process to honestly look at what you say to yourSelf and shift your beliefs. The Soul Stems in this book are a natural process for doing this.

Take time to connect with others in your community or in the online community.

https://www.facebook.com/groups/
IntuitiveMastery/

GUIDELINE FOR HOSTING JOURNAL GROUPS

People are wonderful one at a time. Each one of them has an entire hologram of the universe somewhere within them.

~ George Carlin

AS A YOUNG woman and single mom, I struggled to make the right choices in my life. In hindsight I was able to see where I failed. I used "being confused" as a way of not taking responsibility and action. One of the ways my intuition developed was through my journaling and dream work. I began to understand how to access information from my Higher Self and later connect with Angels and Guides.

My heart's desire is that this book serves as a guide for you to activate your intuition and focus Light on your Shadow side to create health, abundance and joy in your life!

For those who are drawn to create groups and to facilitate this process I am adding this Guideline. My blessing goes to you in this journey. Please support my book by recommending it to your group. There are also audios available at *http://energymedicinedna.com* that correlate with each of the chakras. This is especially helpful in clearing your energy field, understanding the meaning of and clearing the chakras and using the tool of visualization to see your own chakra images.

Preparation for Leading a Group

GROUP SIZE

The group size will depend on your space and your time. If everyone will be sharing, I find eight people works well. The group runs about 2 hours. If you want to have a larger group, you can do the writing exercises and then just have a few people share or do the writing in a large group and break out into smaller groups for sharing. What generally happens in this kind of a group is when one person shares, several others resonate and gain a similar insight. Some people will want to share and others will want to journal and just listen.

PRIVACY AND CONFIDENTIALITY

Take some time to set the group rule of confidentiality. Your particular group can decide what this means. It can be not sharing any information, sharing some information but no names, or sharing who is in the group, but not what is said there.

The *Live Intuitively* Group I facilitate is listed in my Meetup.com group Spirituality. There it is public knowledge who signs up. Some people email me privately to let me know they will be attending.

There will also be people who are afraid to take the journal home, fearing someone may read it. One suggestion is they buy a canvas three ring binder that locks, use a briefcase or use a lockable journal. They could also shred the writing once they are finished. One woman in my group leaves her journal with me. She trusts I would not read it, but she has already shared it in group anyway.

When I facilitate the group I also encourage the members to write for themselves and not for me or the group. Each time they can choose to share or not. They can also share part of what they write and not the rest. As the facilitator I often read some of what I wrote, skipping the parts that I don't want to share.

I ask everyone in the group each time (if there are new people) to agree on the confidentiality and privacy. This creates safety in the group.

Introduction to the Intuitive Reading and Soul Stem Process

GROUNDING MEDITATION

At the beginning of the group start with the Grounding Meditation. Read this to them giving them time to ground and release energy.

> *Close your eyes and take a deep breath from your belly. Pull your aura in around your body six to eight inches. Choose a grounding cord like a waterfall, a beam of light, or a tree trunk. Imagine the grounding cord going down from the base of your spine below your tailbone down through the chair, the floor and through the many layers of earth, all the way down into the fiery center of Mother Earth. Have the grounding cord be fully attached near the base of your spine and fully attached at the center of the Earth.*

> *Starting at the top of your head, release energy from the top of your head all the way down your body and down your grounding cord. The more you do this, the more you will sense the energy and the grounding.*

> *Your body feels safe when you are grounded. The energy that is released can be hurriedness, negative feelings, pain, or other people's energy that has attached to you. Releasing energy down the grounding cord can prevent stress which may prevent illness.*

It is important to practice this grounding as it will become more natural with practice.

If you cannot envision this, that is fine. Just follow along and your body-mind will know what to do.

When you are grounded in present time you are able to manifest better. You cannot manifest when your bodies are in the future. To manifest, you create in your mind, but make sure your body is grounded in present time.

Take another deep breath from your belly and continue release energy down your grounding cord.

After the meditation I ask them to center in their hearts and to get an intention for this particular class.

Have your students get this audio and practice between classes. In the chakra section of the book they will learn to read each chakra and find a symbol to use to journal with

http://energymedicinedna.com/12-minute-energy-clearing-meditation/

The meditation helps people to get centered and present and grounded in their body and ready to access their intuitive self.

CHECK IN

Participants will be sharing their writing, so I keep the check in time to a minimum. You may just have them check in with their name and whether or not they currently journal or journaled since the last group. Check in is not usually necessary. Whatever happened recently generally surfaces in their writing.

READING A CHAPTER

You can either read from the book before the writing exercise or have the group members read ahead of time and come ready to write. My experience is that many people do not prepare for the class, so have them bring their books and read together.

When you are in the Chakra section of this book, you can have them prepare by looking at the Chakras on my website.

http://energymedicinedna.com/ what-are-chakras

Also available on the site are the individual Chakra Audios, one for each chakra and the Chakra Audio Program that has the 12 minute Chakra Clearing Meditation and a 44 minute Chakra recording.

CHOOSING A SOUL STEM

When working in Part One of the book it is good to have everyone write from the same Soul stem. The power of the group experience is that the members will match each other energetically and often similar issues arise. Vibrationally, when in a group, participants are tapped into an expanded consciousness and able to access their Higher Selves and their deeper wisdom more easily. This gives staying focused on the same Soul stem even more value.

When working in the Chakra section when they are using the Soul stems but not intuitively reading themselves, I suggest they choose the sentence stem that scares them the most. This stem will give them the greatest results.

INTUITION

When you facilitate the group, if you are going to lead the students in psychically reading themselves, here are some suggestions.

1. Introduce the chakra that you are going to be working on. Go over the information in the chakra and suggest some ways they may see an image relating to that chakra. For instance for the first chakra and the issue of safety, a image may be someone pulled in toward themselves in a protective, fearful manner, or the opposite may be someone who has their arms raised above their head in an expansive, opening to the world manner.

2. After the Grounding Meditation, have them close their eyes, ground their energy and create a white board about 6 – 8 inches in front of their brown chakra. Ask them to image a symbol on the white board that is representative of the chakra.

3. Have your participants purchase the Mp3 download ahead of time so they can practice.

http://energymedicinedna.com/ audio_downloads/

You can also play the audio in the group and teach them. I have created a mp3 for each chakra. Start with the 12 Minute Energy Clearing Meditation to practice the grounding and centering.

4. Once they have their image, have them write notes about it or draw it in their journal. Next you and others in the group can help them turn the image it into a Soul stem. This is easier if you start with the Soul stems in Part One. You begin to understand the best

way to construct the stem.

Here is an example of one of my own writings during a class I facilitated on the fifth chakra. It was amazingly helpful for me.

The image that I saw was a spider with eight legs. The spider was creating a web and then morphed into a blob with the web encompassing and wrapping up the whole spider.

The Soul Stem I used was

~

THE WEB THAT ENCOMPASSES ME IS . . .

The web that encompasses me is . . . my life, my perfectionism. I have to have it this way or that and then I am monitoring how it SHOULD be, blogging, judging, although I say I don't. I judge how it should be. I hold accountable the SHOULDs and lose sight that although everything probably is mathematically perfect, my small piece of the truth is so small I cannot make any judgments, determinations. I can only be compassionate. So that would not start with me because I am compassionate w/my clients and friends. It's the systems that get me going. They should always run perfectly. I am compassionate w/myself, but I still am a perfectionist and need to allow myself to just be. Systems do break down, people break down or maybe break through. The system that has me crazy is the WWW oh – that's it – the web – Aweber

– and I have done myself in the w/the anger
I have felt over the program.

Then today I could feel that anger coming up when I was on the phone with Katrina. I have to stop blaming people for my lack of understanding, my education and knowledge about a subject and the fact that things break down. What would my life be like if I truly didn't sweat the small stuff? Mostly I don't. I can hold the space for some things that are devastating and I don't react. I realize now where I go into anger – covers up fear = ego is when I hit up against something I don't understand or can't do easily I have been able to skate through life intellectually with ease, but now I am up against things that are beyond my understanding and comprehension w/o a lot of study, effort, work. Oh, poor me, big deal. Candess, you can do this. Be humbled and grateful for what you are learning and the support you have. You have incredible opportunities in your business. Stop Whining!

~

Some backstory on this situation was I used Aweber for my email system. I was in the process of developing and nurturing my clients with emails that empowered them and taught intuitive skills. It was not working right and, finally, two years later, after 9 hours on the phone with Aweber, they agreed there was something wrong and they couldn't figure it out. I since moved to using Infusionsoft, which I love!

Journaling

> *This pouring thoughts out on paper has relieved me.*
> *I feel better and full of confidence and resolution.*

~ Diet Eman

JOURNAL

Most people will bring a journal with them, but I have several on hand just in case. Again, these are spiral notebooks in a variety of colors to choose from that you can get from the office supply store in back-to-school sales for a very inexpensive price. The little girl in me usually buys about 50 every fall and I give them to clients all year long.

PENS

I encourage people to have a fast writing pen that works well. I set out a cup full of pens that I get from Costco. Even if people come with their favorite pen, eventually they give up and use the fast writing pen.

JOURNAL PROCESS

Once they have their Soul stem, set the timer for 10 minutes. When the timer goes off, let them know they can continue to write until they complete their thought or process. When journaling on their own I encourage students to set the timer for 20 minutes.

READING AND SHARING

After the writing process you can either ask who wants to start or have the person on your left start. Rather than waiting for someone to choose to share, I usually have people share going in a circle, one after another. It saves time and gives them the sense of when it will be their turn, which creates safety - a first chakra issue important to any group.

STRUCTURING A SOUL STEM

After the first writing process, to go deeper they create another Soul stem. As the facilitator I assist them in doing this. I usually choose the part of the writing that has a "charge" on it, meaning something that has some emotion, resistance, or some energy to it. If it is difficult to find this next stem from their writing, I suggest they look at the Soul stems I provide. I have them look at what scares them the most and write about that! The goal is to tap into the complex (explained in the introduction) and release it.

When you have a group that becomes bonded, they too will begin to share and help each other to find the best, next Soul stem. This is what I love about this *Live Intuitively* Soul stem process!

After the second journaling session, assist the member to find the next Soul stem to take home and work with. If the issue was resolved they can use some of the Soul stems in the book in between group sessions and share with their accountability partner and in the online group.

CLOSING

At the end of the class, I ask if there is anyone that has something they have to share to be complete. Once this is done, I again take them into the short **Grounding Meditation**, having them ground themselves and release whatever came up for them in the group. I have them focus in their heart and access within themselves whether or not their intention was fulfilled.

Please share with others in the Facebook group how your group is going and what you are learning about yourSelf!

https://www.facebook.com/groups/ IntuitiveMastery/

ACKNOWLEDGMENTS

I OFFER A heartfelt thanks to the women who attended the Intuitive Souls Chakra Journal classes. This was a powerful group of women who shared deeply from their hearts! This sacred group shared their writing and we laughed and cried.

In this safe place I was able to shift through my own shadow and also refine the book and expand the examples that may help you to go deeper.

CONVERSATION WITH CANDESS

When did you first know that you were intuitive?

Realizing that I was intuitive came slowly for me. What really happened was I began to realize that everyone else was not as attuned to their intuition as I was. When you have abilities, you often don't know that others don't have them until situations start to happen. The accuracy of my timeline may be off, but I've journaled most of my life and have 30 years of journals, so when I write my book from my journals I'll be more clear on exact dates.

What catapulted my abilities was when I attended The Church of Divine Man. I would receive chakra readings there and then I immediately was able to read myself. Later I volunteered at an HIV/AIDS retreat with my friend Cheyenne. She provided acupuncture and I did a healing process I had learned through the church. As I was moving energy through the chakras of the retreat participants, I started to see information and get images. I asked if they were interested in the information I got and there was a resounding yes. After spending about six hours doing healings and readings, I became confident in my ability. Later, I began practicing with a friend and we set up classes where we taught the process.

How do I trust intuition when I cannot see it or feel it?

Trusting your intuition is a process. The first step is to understand the Four Ways that you access intuition.

- *Clairaudience*

- *Claircognizance*

- *Clairsentience*

- *Clairvoyance*

You'll begin to understand that you already get intuitive information but it is so illusive that you don't notice. It is the quiet voice, the quiet sense, the quiet knowing, or the fleeting image. Keeping a notebook or journal of your "intuitive hits" and following up on the results will help.

How do I discriminate my intuition from what I really want to be true?

When your intuition is different from what you want to be true, you may sense a resistance. You might think "there's something wrong here" or "this doesn't feel right." Jot down your thoughts and explore them. Have you ever been house shopping and the minute you walked in, you knew it was for you? Think back to what that felt like and use that as an example of what it feels like to be in alignment with your intuition.

How do I value and follow my intuition when the group is choosing another way?

For those of us that are actively intuitive, this happens a lot. If you can influence others in a positive direction, that is great. Often, though, you need to use your intuition to guide yourself and be detached from the group process. In a workshop I took from Caroline Myss, she said when you are in a tribe (group) you move as slowly as the tribe moves. You can connect with the group, but create individually at your own pace.

My friend and Chiropractor Dr. Patrick Dougherty said Candess, you use your intuition all the time as a tool. How do I harness my intuition as a useful tool rather than when it just pops up?

First, review the characteristics of Intuition. There is Clairaudience, Claircognizance, Clairsentience, and Clairvoyance. When I first started becoming aware of my intuition, I used Clairsentience most. Later I developed the others. Choose one that is most natural to you and, when you have an issue you are looking at, start with that ability. Journaling about it can be helpful.

Start with an issue that doesn't have a major consequence, such as choosing a meal at a restaurant rather than something like buying a house. Remember when you were ordering a meal at a restaurant and knew not to order a certain food, thinking that your stomach would not digest it well, but knowing another time you could eat it? Start with this kind of situation and consciously use your intuition when you eat for a few days. Then generalize this ability to other issues.

I often see birds or fish in my readings for myself or others. Is it up to the person that the reading is done for to find the meaning behind the animals or is it up to us to expand on what it is symbolizing?

When I read someone, often symbols come to me that give me meaning and sometimes the same symbol will show up that I am familiar with. For instance, I often see cotton in the fifth chakra that represents someone trying to keep that person from talking. It can also represent someone not being willing to talk. The image of a bird can mean a lot of different things, depending on the bird or the chakra where the bird shows up, and also what the issue is that your client presents. First start with what the bird represents to you and explore that information. You may also ask the client what the bird means to them. I do find when doing this that some people will then get in their heads and get confused and reading them may become more difficult. If you get a sense that it is important for your client to understand their own connection with that bird, I would give them a Soul stem to work on after the reading. It may be "The [name of bird] represents . . ." or "The [name of bird] wants to tell me . . ." or "The [name of bird] guided me by . . ."

Often after I give a reading I tell the person that they may not understand everything I said immediately, but in a couple of days more will come to them through dreams, memory, or their own intuition.

Journaling and owning your intuition can be the breakthrough you have been looking for!

Enjoy the process!

REFERENCED SOURCES & RESOURCES

Caroline Myss, Anatomy of the Spirit: The Seven Stages of Power and Healing (1997)

Caroline Myss, *Medical Intuition Training* (April 2004)

Donna Eden, Balancing your Body's Energy for Optimal Health, Joy and Vitality (2008)

Elizabeth Kubler0-Ross, On Death and Dying: What the Dying Can Teach Doctors, Nurses, Clergy and Their Own Families (1973)

EMDR - Eye Movement Desensitization Reprocessing

http://www.emdr.com

Mary Ellen Flora, Meditation: Key to   Spiritual Awakening.

2nd ed. Everett, WA: CDM Publications. (2000) Periscope

https://www.periscope.tv/

Marc Ragsdale, owner, Prospus

https://prospus.com

The Queen Archetype LiveEncounters Magazine

http://energymedicinedna.com/ the-queen-archetype-2

Sarah Ban Breathnach, *Simple Abundance: A Daybook of Comfort of Joy* (2008)

Wikipedia (**https://www.wikipedia.org**) states from Ruth Snowden's Teach YourSelf Freud, "The ego is the organized part of the personality structure that includes defensive, perceptual, intellectual-cognitive, and executive functions. Conscious awareness resides in the ego, although not all of the operations of the ego are conscious. Originally, Freud used the word ego to mean a sense of self, but later revised it to mean a set of psychic functions such as judgment, tolerance, reality testing, control, planning, defense, synthesis of information, intellectual functioning, and memory. The ego separates out what is real. It helps us to organize our thoughts and make sense of them and the world around us."

Workflowy

https://workflowy.com/invite/2e942af9.lnx

~

Here are some tools resources from **Candess M. Campbell**

Self-Help Toolbox

http://energymedicinedna.com/ self-help-toolbox/

This is connected to *12 Weeks to Self-Healing: Transforming Pain through Energy Medicine* and will provide you with several tools.

DNA Activation, etc

http://energymedicinedna.com/

Anxiety Assessment

http://energymedicinedna.com/ self-help-toolbox/

Depression Assessment

http://energymedicinedna.com/ self-help-toolbox/

Candess's Youtube channel which contains videos that will assist you in developing your intuition

*https://www.youtube.com/user/
EnergyMedicineDNA*

ABOUT THE AUTHOR

CANDESS M. CAMPBELL, PhD is the author of the #1 Best-selling book *12 Weeks to Self-Healing: Transforming Pain through Energy Medicine*[3]. She is an internationally known Speaker, Intuitive Coach and Mentor, and Psychic Medium.

She has her doctorate in Clinical Hypnotherapy from American Pacific University. Her Master's Degree is in Counseling Psychology from Gonzaga University and her Bachelor's Degree is in Psychology with a minor in Religious Studies, also from Gonzaga.

She specializes in assisting conscious seekers to unleash their highest potential and live a life of abundance, happiness, and joy.

MY STORY

THIS IS THE beginning of it all and so I am a little surprised I would list this at the end, but I think that telling this story is important.

When I was 14 years old I was what was referred to back then as a "Jesus Freak." If you research the movement you will get a lot of different views, but for me it was amazing. There was a coffee house in downtown Spokane called the "I AM Coffeehouse." I hitchhiked downtown from the north side of Spokane to hang out and pass out the newspapers called "The Truth." We shared the message, which was called Witnessing. Today if someone did this, it would annoy me, but this was the late 1960s and early 1970s and a totally different time.

On January 1, 1970 my family was visiting my aunt, uncle, and cousins who lived near Shadle Park. From their house I decided to take the bus downtown to "witness." I walked to the bus stop at Alberta and Rowan and waited. A man pulled up in a baby blue pickup truck and asked me if I wanted a ride. I thought to myself, "Jesus will protect me," so I got in.

I noticed he was taking me somewhere other than downtown. I began to panic and I could hardly breathe. I put my hand on the door handle, contemplating my next move. The truck turned left and I quickly opened the door and either jumped or flew out - or both.

The next thing I remember was waking to bright lights overhead. My eyes focused and I saw my dad and my mom looking over me, their faces gray and drained. Later I realized I was at Holy Family Hospital. Apparently, I had been in a coma for two weeks.

I was told I had a contusion and a Catholic priest (my dad's faith) had been called and administered last rights. What happened for me, though, was that I experienced floating upwards and going towards a light. There was a being near the light (who now I believe to be Saint Germaine) who said to me, "You are not done yet, you have to go back."

Years later, with the help of my dear friend, the late Dr. Gilbert Milner, I was able to piece together the memories and sensations of this experience. Gil was a psychiatrist, shaman, and hypnotherapist and - through hypnotherapy - he guided me to relive the experience of the accident.

This trauma resulted in brain damage (my term) and I had to relearn to coordinate my body. During the time that my brain was healing, I could not think well and therefore accessed the intuitive part of me in order to survive. This experience catapulted my psychic abilities and somehow left an opening for me to access the world beyond the physical.

Since I was a little girl I often reached out for the Spirit world as a safe haven. Although I adored my dad, he was alcoholic and when he was drinking I didn't feel safe. I began to "connect upward" rather than to trust those in physical bodies. I enjoyed a sense of belonging with God and the Angels and today I work closely with and am guided by a group of Ascended Masters called the Lords of Karma.

INDEX

Made in the USA
Charleston, SC
27 June 2016